The Everything Anxiety-Coping Book!

Transforming Anxiety into a Positive Force

© 2010 By: James M. Lowrance

TABLE OF CONTENTS:

SECTION ONE - "A Complete Look at Anxiety Disorders"

CHAPTERS:

The Everything Anxiety-Coping Book!

SECTION TWO - "The Best Darn Anxiety Disorders Book!"

CHAPTERS:

1. 40 Million U.S. Adult Anxiety Disorder Sufferers
2. Understanding the Fight or Flight Response
3. Medical Causes of Anxiety Symptoms
4. Anxiety Disorder Symptom Phenomena
5. More about Chronic Anxiety Unreality Symptoms
6. Obsessive-Compulsive Disorder - Basic Facts
7. Post Traumatic Stress Disorder Basic Facts
8. Panic Disorder Basic Information
9. Generalized Anxiety Disorder Basic Facts
10. Social Anxiety Disorder Basic Facts
11. Chronic Thoughts of Irrational Worry
12. Dealing with a Climax of Anxiety Symptoms
13. When the Stress of Life becomes Overwhelming

The Everything Anxiety-Coping Book!

The Everything Anxiety-Coping Book!

SECTION THREE - "Treatments for Medically Caused Anxiety and Depression"

CHAPTERS:

1. More about Medical Causes of Anxiety
2. More about Panic Disorder and Thyroid Disease
3. Anxiety with Thyroid Hormone Therapy
4. Medical Causes of Depression
5. Is "Nervous Breakdown" a True Medical Term?
6. Coping Methods for Anxiety Disorders and Major Depression

SECTION FOUR - "Identifying and Treating Mental and Emotional Disorders"

CHAPTERS:

1. The Differences Between Psychosis and Common Anxiety and Depression
2. Cognitive Behavioral Therapy for Anxiety Disorders
3. The Basic Differences between Anxiety & Depression
4. Antidepressants Effective for some but not for Others
5. More Patent Education and Doctor Communication about SSRI Antidepressants
6. Stress Management to Aid Treatments for Mind and Emotions

The Everything Anxiety-Coping Book!

INTRODUCTION:

This book containing 36-chapters, is a compilation of four previously published titles that have been combined into one comprehensive resource. The subjects covered include aspects of Anxiety Disorders, their symptom manifestations, coping methods and treatments. It is my hope that readers will find this book to be a valuable resource for personal anxiety coping or for that in supporting their loved ones who suffer chronic anxiety.

(NOTE: Some information within the different sections that will follow, is repeated to some degree but each chapter was written as a unique article originally and each contains unique perspectives.)

The Everything Anxiety-Coping Book!

SECTION ONE - "A Complete Look at Anxiety Disorders"

Chapter 1.
<u>Chapter 1.</u>

The True Purpose of Anxiety

The main focus within the following chapters is to help anxiety sufferers learn not to fear the symptoms of anxiety. This is an aspect of "Cognitive Behavioral Therapy" (CBT) that, in my opinion is the single most effective one that contributes toward overcoming anxiety disorders. I will also discuss the importance of stress-reduction because added stressors can result in a condition referred to as "anxiety sensitization".

Anxiety is natural and one of the most common emotions we all experience.

Without the anxiety mechanism, we might not have the sudden "presence of mind" and the sudden increased ability to react and jump out of the way of an oncoming truck that is barreling down the street, on a direct path to run over us! This mechanism, called the "fight or flight response", that gives us the extra strength and energy to fight or run, is designed to protect us and so in situations like these (to use a cliche), "anxiety is our friend".

Anxiety also helps us when we have tasks to perform. People who perform as actors in Broadway plays or have important public speeches to make or a Fireman who has a fire to put out etc..., all depend on the fight or flight response, to enhance their performance and to provide them that added inspiration for the task at hand, so again in cases like these, anxiety is our friend.

Symptoms of Anxiety

Anxiety symptoms generally include the following.

- *apprehension*

- *worry*

- *feelings of fear*

- *rapid heart beat*

- *hyperventilation*

- *excessive sweating*

- *blushing*

- *trembling*

- *increased blood pressure*

- *muscle tension*

- *an urge to escape*

The Everything Anxiety-Coping Book!

These symptoms are included in what are called "anxiety disorders" and are experienced to varying degrees, depending upon which anxiety disorder a person may be experiencing. The chapters that follow will help us to identify different types of common anxiety disorders.

Chapter 2.

When is Anxiety Considered a Disorder?

Disordered anxiety can cause fears and phobias to develop and to cause ordinary situations to become avoided by the one experiencing them. One example of anxiety that develops into a "disorder" is when a person becomes fearful of social situations and settings. A certain degree of anxiety is normal in social settings because it actually lends toward a respectful attitude and helps us to put our best foot forward when making friends and acquaintances but when shyness becomes extreme and a full-blown fear, the anxiety then becomes a disorder.

Another way to look at this is to say that under normal circumstances, anxiety happens in the "order" it is supposed to. Unfortunately in some people, the anxiety "fight or flight response", begins to trigger at the inappropriate times or in a "disordered" fashion.

Anything that can be labeled "disordered", must also have the ability to be in the "correct order" (appropriately ordered).

The way in which anxiety can become a "disordered" thing, is when it does not happen at the appropriate time or is "out of the order" in which it was meant to be. This does not make the anxiety itself an unnatural thing, only the timing becomes unnatural! Anxiety becomes "Anxiety Disorder", when a person has developed learned behaviors, that causes it to activate more often than it should or due to things that have become triggers for anxiety that normally should not be.

Triggers are also called "phobias", meaning simply "fears" of various different things. Some people develop more fears, due to the anxiety reaction itself. The fight or flight response to specific things can be experienced and perceived as "negative" by a person and they will then have that negative type of response to that same experience/trigger, repeatedly, until they are able to overcome that fear/phobia.

The Everything Anxiety-Coping Book!

Other persons exposed to those same triggers, might have positive anxiety reactions to them, that we might actually call "positive excitement".

An example of this might be a person who becomes, phobic around snakes and their anxiety response feels very negative to them when seeing a snake and this triggers their phobia. Another person who loves seeing and being around snakes, might instead become curiously excited and have just as powerful an adrenaline surge (fight or flight response), when seeing a snake but instead of it causing them to run away from the snake, it makes them want to chase after it and catch it. This is not such a ridiculous example because I have a nephew, who when he was a child, caught many snakes and other unusual creatures and loved every minute of it, despite being bitten a few times!

The point of this look at the term "disorder", as related to anxiety, is so that we can better understand that anxiety can be used positively or negatively in our lives.

The Everything Anxiety-Coping Book!

No one has anxiety mastered to the point that it works for them positively in every situation they experience but it gives each of us a goal in life, to learn to channel anxiety into positive energy as often as we possibly can. We can also work on those phobias, to try and change them into positive experiences, so that the negative feelings begin to fade (this is easier said than done and it does take practice). One person can experience an adrenaline surge as a very negative experience, such as someone who has a negative panic reaction to a roller coaster ride, while another person on the same ride will have just as strong an adrenaline reaction but will experience it as fun and exciting!

People with Anxiety Disorders should be encouraged to know that with help through treatments, such as "Cognitive Behavioral Therapy" and other positive treatments and therapies they can learn over time, to change those learned behaviors so that more anxiety reactions, become positive rather than negative experiences.

The Everything Anxiety-Coping Book!

Chapter 3.

Four Common Anxiety Disorders

Generalized Anxiety Disorder (GAD): This common anxiety disorder manifests with chronic worry as a major symptom. It affects an estimated 6.8 million Americans and affects twice as many adult women as men. People with this anxiety disorder find themselves worrying intensely and continually about everyday issues, such as work, relationships, school and health. While most people worry to a degree about these same issues, people with GAD do so to an exaggerated extent and on an ongoing basis (chronic). The worry aspect of this anxiety disorder also involves unrealistic or irrational worries as well, such as having constant concern over "what might happen", even if the chances are that the things being worried about will not happen. This type of worry over irrational concerns is also sometimes referred to as "what if thinking" and is also a feature of other anxiety disorders.

The Everything Anxiety-Coping Book!

According to some mental health sources, a person must have this type of severe worrying for at least six months for it to be considered as a possibility for being Generalized Anxiety Disorder.

Social Anxiety Disorder (SAD): We all have a degree of apprehension when it comes to meeting new people or attending social events and settings. People with SAD will have an exaggerated fear of socializing, which is also referred to as "social phobia." With this anxiety disorder, shyness becomes extreme and causes the person to begin to avoid social situations and to become extremely anxious when they are required to attend such events or to meet new people, even when it is individuals rather than a group.

People with social anxiety disorder find themselves experiencing heightened anxiety symptoms in social settings, such as feelings of panic, excessive sweating, trembling and hyperventilation (rapid breathing).

The Everything Anxiety-Coping Book!

Much of what brings on these symptoms in people with SAD is the fear of being judged by others who are observing them or of looking silly or stupid in from of them. This phobia, affecting 15 million American adults, causes them to avoid social events and settings.

Panic Disorder (PD): The majority of Americans have had a panic reaction to some type of event at some time in their lives. But for 6 million American adults, panic reactions or "panic attacks" begin to trigger on a continual basis. This indicates the development of panic disorder. Having an occasional panic attack does not point to panic disorder but if a person has a panic attack every day or several a day, this strongly indicates that the disorder has developed. For many people with panic disorder, it was the original panic attack that then causes them to experience more of them. Because the original attack was so unpleasant, the fear (phobia) of having additional panic attacks serves as a trigger for causing them afterward.

Panic attacks include all of the symptoms listed previously in chapter one but with panic, the symptoms happen forcefully and suddenly and create what might be referred to as a "climax" of anxiety.

Post Traumatic Stress Disorder (PTSD): This anxiety disorder results from experiences that are extremely traumatizing to a person. Once the event has taken place, the person is unable to fully recover from it emotionally. The event that triggers PTSD can be an act of violence perpetrated upon them or witnessed by them, a severe accident that causes severe shock or a sudden loss of a loved one. The person with PTSD will often relive the traumatic event by having it replay repeatedly in their mind. This replay may not be voluntary but simply a deeply embedded memory they cannot shake from their subconscious. A PTSD sufferer will also sometimes experience nightmares relating to the traumatic event or possibly even experience flashbacks that cause them to believe they are actually reliving the event repeatedly.

War veterans who are traumatized while fighting in combat duty, will commonly experience this anxiety disorder. An estimated 7.7 million Americans suffer from PTSD.

More detail will be given to descriptions of these anxiety disorders and to the distinguishing, characteristic features of each in the section titled "The Best Darn Anxiety Disorder E-Book!" that will follow this section.

Chapter 4.

Anxiety Sensitization

There is a phase that most anxiety suffers are very familiar with having experienced, as part of their anxiety condition, called; "Anxiety Sensitization". This is a state of sensitivity an anxiety sufferer can reach, when they have experienced an extra amount of stress over a period of time and it causes them to reach a heightened state of being sensitive to anxiety feelings. When a person reaches this stage of heightened sensitivity to anxiety, they will experience anxiety reactions more easily. Anxiety responses to things will also be more easily triggered while in this state.

An anxiety sufferer who reaches this state of sensitivity, may become concerned that they have entered a more severe stage of anxiety disorder.

The Everything Anxiety-Coping Book!

These phases however, are almost certain to be temporary increases in the anxiety condition and not a permanent worsening of the condition. Once they can achieve relief from their added stressors, they will often see the sensitivity diminish.

When a person is extra tired or extra stressed, they have less resistance to any negative feelings and medical research states that there is also less resistance to physical illnesses when one is stressed-out. Most anxiety sufferers can likely also relate to the fact, that when you are physically weak from an illness or feeling extra tired, this can also cause anxiety to be triggered more easily because one is in a less resistant state.

People with anxiety conditions, should observe those times when they reach this state of becoming sensitized to anxiety, so that they can learn to reverse some of the trends that lend toward getting stressed out.

The Everything Anxiety-Coping Book!

For example; if staying involved in mental studies, such as being on the computer for too long or doing paper work, such as tax returns for extended periods, results in feeling stressed out and sensitized to anxiety, a person needs to learn to pace their self instead of taking on too much of these type activities at a time. It is also a good idea not to take on too many duties at once (multi-tasking), in trying to get them all accomplished too quickly. This too is a stress-producer and one should instead be looking for stress-reducers.

Some ideas for stress-reducing, in addition to the things mentioned above, would be to take time out to do things that are enjoyable and pleasurable. If one enjoys being outdoors to observe all of the natural beauty and fresh air, then they should take time out of their duties and take a nature walk or just sit under a shade tree, with a glass of decaffeinated tea and relax.

If exercise is a stress reducer for a person (and it is for many people), then leave they should leave their duties behind for a while and get some exercise. This should be done as often as needed to keep stress levels down, as long as one does not exceed their tolerance level for exercise.

Persons with Generalized Anxiety Disorder, tend to be the type of anxiety sufferers who push themselves too hard and try to get too many things done in unreasonably short periods of time. This is often due to their worries about things getting piled up on them, if they don't stay ahead of their duties. Gad sufferers also stay busy, because it helps them experience some relief from their constant worry and free-floating anxiety feelings. This trend however, can also end in periods of feeling stressed out, so that there is a vicious cycle of seeking stress relief that instead actually results in causing excessive stress.

People with Gad and other anxiety conditions should work on these methods for reducing stress but should also not become overly concerned if they should reach one of these stressed out phases, that causes them to be sensitized to anxiety. The phase will pass and afterward, another opportunity will present itself to again work on eliminating the trends that lead to these phases.

It is also important for anxiety sufferers to remember that if they do reach the point of anxiety sensitization, it will not cause them insanity, or death from intense, ongoing periods of anxiety. Adrenaline, the major anxiety producing hormone, can only reach a certain level of effect and then can go no further. The human body is designed so that it will only utilize a certain amount of adrenaline at a time because it can only metabolize that amount at any given time. The sensations from being overly-adrenalized are unpleasant but they will pass, given time.

The Everything Anxiety-Coping Book!

It is important to work on stress-reducing techniques, incorporating exercise, deep-breathing techniques (slow diaphramic breathing, inflating the stomach rather than the chest) and any other methods that one knows will help them to avoid or reduce those stressed out phases that lead to becoming sensitized to anxiety. With time, it can help one to overcome and conquer negative anxiety experiences in their life.

Chapter 5.

Catastrophic Thinking

A young lady recently e-mailed me after reading one of my online articles on an anxiety subject, asking if having bizarre thoughts about terrible things was common with severe anxiety states. I assured her that these type thoughts were indeed common to anxiety sufferers and that the name for them is "catastrophic thinking".

She described to me, that when severe anxiety states occurred with her, she would have racing thoughts, many of them having to do with the fear of losing control and hurting herself, or others and sometimes the thought included that of even harming her own baby. This was understandably very concerning to her because like many anxiety sufferers, she believed these violent, sadistic and tragic type thoughts indicated that she was on the verge of losing her sanity.

The Everything Anxiety-Coping Book!

The fact is however, that catastrophic thinking happens commonly with anxiety sufferers and many people refer to it as "what if thinking". Anxiety Disorder patients describe thoughts like the above ones, that the young lady described but these can also include other fearful thoughts such as thinking one will lose control in front of other people and make a complete fool of their self. Other anxiety patients may have thoughts of passing out and needing an ambulance, but not being in a location where others will notice and call for help. Others describe thoughts of snapping and becoming violent to others around them or of running down a supermarket isle, screaming at the top of their lungs.

One of the reasons catastrophic thinking is so unpleasant, other than for the reasons already stated, is because these thoughts will increase and intensify already present anxiety conditions. Catastrophic thinking in fact, can be a trigger for panic attacks.

These "what if thoughts", tend to lead from one to another until multiple fearful thoughts are all happening at once, which could be refer to as the "snowball effect". The thoughts gain momentum and loom larger and scarier to the sufferer, as they increase during anxiety states.

Why are these catastrophic type thoughts so common to anxiety sufferers? According to anxiety researchers, they believe, these thoughts happen because the "fight or flight response", will trigger a mechanism having to do with our thought processes, which begins to scan for possible dangers. Of course with anxiety disorders, there are no real dangers that are eminent and so the mind will tend to consider possibilities for why the body is reacting as it is, by triggering the fight or flight response. This scanning for dangers, is actually part of the protection mechanism meant to keep us safe however, the person experiencing them will misinterpret this as meaning they will actually act on these thoughts and fulfill them.

The Everything Anxiety-Coping Book!

Let me assure you that this is not the case with anxiety-induced catastrophic thoughts. The fact that the thoughts are scary to you in-itself is proof that you do not wish to act on them. Someone who is actually considering such actions will actually take pleasure in these type thoughts when contemplating them, rather than fearing them and resisting them. These type thoughts are very common to anxiety disorder sufferers and do not in any way indicate that one is losing their sanity or actually about to snap and go out of control.

The best way to overcome the fear of such thoughts which will in turn also cause them to fade away and stop happening is to reassure one's self of these facts. I have read the testimonials of anxiety sufferers who actually learned to see humor in these thoughts, rather than being terrified of them and this resulted in catastrophic thinking, losing its power in their lives. This is of course easier said than done but with time and repeated reassuring of one's self it can be accomplished with very good results.

The Everything Anxiety-Coping Book!

When you think about it, these type thoughts can actually be humorous and one might even add a little humor to them, as they begin happening! For example, if one has a fear of losing control, they can add to that thought, the idea of climbing a tree and hanging from a limb, upside down by their legs. This might sound like a ridiculous method but it can be as effective as any other method, in diverting these type thoughts and getting them more under control.

A final bit of advice I would give however, is not to make it a fight or struggle any more than one has to, instead they should almost make a little game out of it, or see it as an interesting experiment because anxiety seems to thrive on struggle. Once one gains ground on catastrophic thinking, they will see the struggle aspect of gaining control of their thoughts, fade away and over time it will automatically be replaced with pleasant, positive thoughts and thinking.

Chapter 6.

Depersonalization and Derealization

There is a common symptom-phenomenon anxiety disorder sufferers will experience, called "depersonalization and de-realization". These occur commonly in patients with anxiety disorder and sometimes also in those with clinical depression, who suffer from co-existing anxiety and can be very concerning to them. What I wish to do within this chapter is to explain what these symptoms are and to offer some comfort to those who may suffer Anxiety Disorders by relating the fact that both of these categories of unreality symptoms are experienced commonly with these emotional disorders and in the vast majority of cases, they are neither harmful nor dangerous.

Depersonalization

This symptom phenomenon commonly found in anxiety disorder sufferers but especially in those with panic attacks, is a symptom-induced experience in which a patient feels as if they are "unreal" and like they no longer exist as a person. They may even feel they have become invisible and that others around them are real but they no longer are. Some patients describe it as feeling like being a robot and no longer like a human being. Patients have described episodes for example of looking at their own hand in front of their face and wondering if it is really there. Patients will also describe experiences of looking into a mirror and actually feeling as if they do not recognize themselves and they feel as if they are possibly having some type of identity crisis. Obviously, these are very scary and very unpleasant experiences for anxiety patients and ones they certainly do not want to continue or to reoccur.

These episodes of depersonalization are reported by some anxiety disorder sufferers, to happen immediately preceding the onset of a panic attack or with other severe anxiety symptoms, while others experience depersonalization during an attack of severe anxiety or panic symptoms. Once the depersonalization symptom is experienced by some anxiety suffers, they report that it will occur more frequently and will be triggered more easily afterward, even with less severe anxiety symptoms being present.

Derealization

This aspect of unreality symptoms is similar but in this case, that which seems to become unreal is the person's surroundings. With de-realization, an anxiety sufferer will have episodes of experiencing feelings that their surroundings have become unreal. They will feel as if even reality itself is no longer something they can fully grasp during those moments but this is simply a sensation and they are not actually losing touch with reality.

The Everything Anxiety-Coping Book!

They may even question the existence of things and wonder if life itself is a dream of some type. Some descriptions I have heard of this experience are described as feeling like "being inside of a bubble", or "like trying to see everything through a curtain" and "like everything is covered with a thick fog".

Many anxiety sufferers will experience both depersonalization and de-realization at the same time or these may alternate, so that they experience each one at different times. During episodes of either, they will also commonly experience mind fog, meaning they feel hazy and unable to fully concentrate. These features only add to the unpleasantness of these experiences.

What causes these strange feelings of depersonalization and de-realization that are so concerning to anxiety sufferers?

Well we know that the "fight or flight response" itself is a protection mechanism, created in us to help us flee or to fight danger and to help us perform more powerfully, when important tasks are at hand. These unreality type symptoms, in which things seem to become unreal is very likely part of that same protection mechanism. It may be that our minds will cause ourselves and our surroundings, to temporarily fade from our minds and into the background, in order for us to concentrate more intensely on locating any actual danger that threatens us, whether real or imagined. It is similar to the reason an anxiety patient's mind will race at times because it is trying to scan for dangers that have threatened them and that are setting off the fight or flight response. We also know that physical senses are heightened during strong anxiety responses and this-too likely adds to these feelings of unreality.

What is important for anxiety sufferers to know and to understand is the fact that these unreality symptoms do not indicate the onset of insanity or of one losing their mind.

The Everything Anxiety-Coping Book!

They are very common occurrences with anxiety conditions and will not cause damage to a person's mind or sanity. The fear of going crazy is a very common and concerning one to those who experience severe anxiety episodes and also to those with clinical depression and these two often co-exist but these are irrational thoughts and will not take place.

True Psychosis

Psychosis is the term for one actually losing touch with reality and having delusions and hallucinations. It is the term for actual mental disorders that may or may not have significant emotional aspects to them. Anxiety and common clinical depression are both in the neurosis category, meaning they are stress related and not caused by an underlying mental disorder. Persons with severe forms of depression, such as Bipolar Disorder, may have psychotic episodes but the more common type depression, called Clinical or Major Depression, is not in the psychosis category.

The Everything Anxiety-Coping Book!

Estimates by some Mental Health Organizations state that psychosis affects an estimated 1% of the U.S. population, whereas the more common anxiety and depression conditions affect a much higher percent of the population (some place the statistic at exceeding 40%).

Patients with severe anxiety conditions need to learn not to fear these unreality type symptoms because adding more fear will intensify and extend the duration of these episodes. This is of course more easily said than done but with time and effort, those with Anxiety Disorders can learn to have less fear of these unreality symptoms so that the symptoms are what fade into the background rather than the realities of self and surroundings.

If you are an anxiety and/or depression sufferer and are concerned by these unreality type symptoms, I recommend conducting a search online if possible, using the search term "Anxiety De-realization and Depersonalization".

The Everything Anxiety-Coping Book!

You will find many resource articles stating facts in regard to how common these unreality symptoms are and the fact that they are not harmful or dangerous. In fact another search, using another search term: "Anxiety Depersonalization and De-realization, neither harmful nor dangerous" will yield even more articles that will help in this area. These unreality symptoms are very commonly experienced and not dangerous, although extremely unpleasant.

Chapter 7.

Calming Yourself during Panic Attacks or Severe Anxiety Episodes

A panic attack is a climax of anxiety symptoms that causes them to be experienced suddenly and forcefully.

The symptoms may include the following.

• intense fear

• rapid heart rate

• hyperventilation

• an urge to escape

• muscle tension

• dizziness

• sweating

• mild to moderate pain/pressure in the chest

The Everything Anxiety-Coping Book!

People, who experience frequent panic attacks, have a condition referred to as Panic Disorder". The following four steps which are often used in different variations of Cognitive Behavioral Therapy techniques (CBT) can help those who suffer panic attacks, to calm their selves when experiencing them.

Remind yourself during a panic attack, that you will not drop dead or lose your sanity.

While panic attacks are the most unpleasant type of anxiety that can be experienced, reputable mental health sources state that they do not lead to loss of sanity, strokes or heart attacks, in otherwise healthy people. Anxiety is a normal mechanism, designed to give the body increased strength to escape danger or to fight an enemy should situations arise requiring the need to do so. It is also designed to help us accomplish urgent or important duties that life might present to us. Panic attacks are an example of this important mechanism, occurring "out of context" meaning they are triggered at times when there is no actual need for the "fight or flight" response.

The Everything Anxiety-Coping Book!

While this improper timing makes panic attacks extremely unpleasant, they are still a normal response the body is designed to experience without causing injury to the mind or body.

The real damage chronic anxiety conditions result-in is restricting some of the freedom and enjoyments of life rather than actually causing mental or physical damage. Reminding yourself of these simple facts, can help diminish the effects of a panic attack and lend toward calming yourself down during one.

Focus on the task you are involved in rather than focusing on the panic attack symptoms.

While this step is certainly easier said than done, with practice, you can learn to divert your attention away from the unpleasant anxiety symptoms and direct your focus more on accomplishing an immediate goal at hand.

The triggers that cause a panic attacks can be simple things such as waiting in line to be checked out at a grocery store or walking to the front isle of a theater to be seated.

Other times things that cause panic attacks are of more importance and significance, such as standing before an audience to make an important speech or rescuing someone from a burning home. Regardless of the tasks needing performed, you can practice focusing more on accomplishing them than on the panic symptoms they may be triggering. This will channel your attention toward your energy in performing these tasks, rather than upon surviving the anxiety symptoms that are attempting to challenge you.

If you feel panic symptoms arising while being checked out at the grocery line, you might consider focusing intently on the magazines or other items near the checkout stand.

When your groceries are being checked out, you might consider mentally calculating the total cost of your groceries to see how close you come to the final tally. If it helps to join in with the clerk in bagging the groceries, you might consider this as a diversion from focusing on anxiety symptoms.

Any method that helps you divert your attention and energy into a task rather than focusing on the anxiety is acceptable and you can also make a game out of it, so that you look forward to the gains you will make over time and actually begin to enjoy accomplishing these goals.

Realize that you are not alone in experiencing panic attacks and that they are not a sign of weakness.

Panic attacks are experienced by an estimated 6 million Americans or about 1 out of every 75.

Mental health professionals who study anxiety disorders, including panic attacks have found that people who suffer chronic anxiety are many times the more creative and passionate people in our society. Famous sports figures including pro football players Earl Campbell and Ricky Williams have suffered panic attacks, as well as famous celebrities including Howie Mandel and Oprah Winfrey.

This places people who suffer panic attacks and panic disorder in good company with some of our nation's most ambitious people. By reminding yourself that greatly admired and creative people suffer chronic anxiety conditions, you can also view yourself as among the most creative and passionate people of our society.

Channel your anxiety into a positive and creative process.

Many anxiety sufferers have found that when they feel on edge or as if they are on the verge of experiencing a panic attack, they are also at their most creative and passionate level. By taking that anxiety energy and channeling it into positive actions, you can redirect it away from negative experiences. Rather than running from the anxiety symptoms or attempting to escape from them when they occur, try channeling that energy into creating something you enjoy.

If you enjoy sculpting, writing or painting, allow the anxiety to trigger your creative juices into flowing by concentrating that energy into those creative arts. If you enjoy sports such as soccer, tennis or martial arts, channel that anxiety energy into improving upon your skills and techniques in these areas.

If you are involved in something or in a location where this is not possible to actually practice these pastimes when anxiety symptoms occur, you might attempt to mentally play the sport in your mind or carry a small notepad for jotting down notes on how you can improve in the sport when you are able to play again.

The Everything Anxiety-Coping Book!

While the following final-suggestion for this step might seem unusual, I will mention that there is a UK website that recently reported that a PhD Stress Management Expert in the U.S. found that anxiety and stress relief can be experienced using romantic and sexual fantasy as an anxiety diversion technique.

In his research, he found that people who conjure torrid fantasies involving romantic and sexual scenarios have found that it helps them to divert negative anxiety responses into passionate imagination with positive results. I would also add the suggestion that you use your spouse and life partner as the object of your fantasies, which will improve both your anxiety symptoms and your love life at the same time.

These are examples of things that can help to diminish the effects of anxiety symptoms and can also help those who suffer panic attacks, to redirect their anxiety into a positive rather than into a negative direction and outcome.

The Everything Anxiety-Coping Book!

Chapter 8.

Is Anxiety Dangerous to Your Health?

Anxiety of itself is never a direct "cause" of strokes or heart attacks but if you are predisposed to having a stroke due to already present health problems such as severe hypertension, it can be a contributing factor or rarely, a trigger for these. I state this fact which comes from much research I've read by PhD MDs and Psychiatrists over the past several years.

The anxiety "flight or flight" response temporarily elevates bodily functions; heart rate, blood pressure, respiration and sweating, the same way exercise does, which can also be potentially dangerous for people with already existing health-risks but it does not pose a danger to otherwise healthy people.

The Everything Anxiety-Coping Book!

Anxiety itself is a natural emotion and is designed to be triggered often if needed without resulting in physically harmful effects. Anxiety is not stress but a "bodily reaction to stress" or what we might see as a pressure valve in a sense or the body's way of dealing-with and utilizing stress.

The hormone - adrenaline/epinephrine that occurs naturally in the body has a limited effect or a cut off level of strength as mentioned previously and it is counteracted by the hormone "noradrenaline" (also called "nor-epinephrine" -- the calming hormone). It is metabolized by the body in such a way, that it cannot continue to escalate to extremely high levels and cause death or severe health effects, in otherwise healthy people. If it could, people would be dropping dead from anxiety left and right every day because statistics state that up to 25% (1 in 4) people have an anxiety problem/disorder at some point in their lives and for a large percent of these people, it is chronic.

The Everything Anxiety-Coping Book!

If anxiety frequently caused severe health problems, we could then say that God or nature has made an error in giving us this protection mechanism.

My purpose in pointing this out is to differentiate from the idea that anxiety "causes" rather than in some cases "contributes" to severe health problems. Anxiety among many other things, can contribute to all kinds of health problems but in most of these conditions, it is not a direct cause of them.

One aspect of anxiety is "worry" however, since everyone on earth with very few exceptions, has worry, it has to be severe and chronic (ongoing) to be classified as an anxiety disorder. This type of chronic anxiety can contribute to a variety of health problems as well (i.e. stomach disorders, hives, headaches, etc...) because it does increase bodily functions, but more subtly than do panic reactions.

While some people may believe confusing these terminologies (recognizing direct causes as opposed to contributing factors) is not that important, it really is because in some cases it results in wrong diagnoses of proposed causes for health problems, etc... It probably sounds like "semantics" or "playing with words" but it's really not and in my opinion people should know the difference.

As previously stated, increased adrenaline over long periods of time, does contribute to serious health problems, such as hypertension and high cholesterol that can then directly cause heart problems and stroke, so these latter mentioned health problems (i.e. hypertension and elevated cholesterol) are the direct causes, while anxiety can be a contributing factor but in most cases not a direct cause.

Anxiety doesn't cause these problems in all people some anxiety sufferers don't develop hypertension or high cholesterol from prolonged anxiety.

The Everything Anxiety-Coping Book!

Like everyone else, anxiety sufferers need to incorporate daily exercise into their routine and improved diet practices because this alone can offset any harmful effects from prolonged anxiety which can contribute to hypertension and elevated cholesterol as mentioned above.

It is important in my opinion, for people with anxiety disorders, especially those who experience panic attacks, to know that the harmful effects of anxiety are almost never immediate unless as previously stated, there are co-existing, serious health problems also present. By believing anxiety – a natural emotion, is so very harmful in otherwise healthy individuals, it makes it very difficult for these patients to learn not to fear any immediate effects from anxiety. Learning not fear anxiety symptoms is a major feature of Cognitive Behavioral Therapy (CBT) but is an aspect patients will have little benefit from if they are told that anxiety will directly cause them, strokes, heart attacks or sudden death.

All anxiety disorders are treatable through various different therapies, including methods of Cognitive Behavioral Therapy that have been discussed in the preceding chapters. Anti-anxiety and anti-depressant medications can also help to alleviate and diminish anxiety symptoms when these are needed. These drugs can also be combined with psychiatric therapies such as CBT and other therapies, for added benefit and in some cases may only be needed temporarily, as short-term treatments.

Types of as-needed anti-anxiety medications (benzodiazepines) include the following:

• alprazolam (Xanax®)

• clonazepam (Klonipin®)

• lorazepam (Ativan®)

• diazepam (Valium®)

• buspirone (Buspar®) (this one is a azaspirodecanedione class drug)

The Everything Anxiety-Coping Book!

Types of anti-depressants (selective serotonin reuptake inhibitors) that also work as anti-anxiety medications include the following:

• paroxetine (Paxil®)

• venlafexine (Effexor®)

• fluoxetine (Prozac®)

• setraline (Zoloft®)

• fluvoxamine (Luvox ®)

If you suspect that you might have a chronic anxiety condition, see your doctor for further evaluation and referral to proper treatments.

Section Two: **The Best Darn Anxiety Disorder Book**

<u>Chapter 1.</u>

40 Million U.S. Adult Anxiety Disorder Sufferers

Chronic Anxiety that Affects up to 20% of the U.S. Population

Anxiety Disorders are the most common emotional disorders affecting Americans as well as people in all countries worldwide but there are effective treatments available.

Millions of Americans suffer a chronic anxiety disorder of some type, at some point during their lifetimes. Severe anxiety is the most common emotional disorder worldwide, with depression coming in at a close second-place. Anxiety and depression often co-exist, which can worsen the symptoms of each.

The Everything Anxiety-Coping Book!

The symptoms of anxiety can be terrifying and sometimes debilitating but there are effective treatments to help with coping and recovery.

Causes of Anxiety Conditions and Disorders

According to the U.S. National Institute of Mental Health (NIMH), anxiety disorders can be related to other mental/emotional disorders, including depression and traumatic or stressful events. They can also be related to physical illnesses that can act as triggers for the development of them or as a contributing factor for ongoing anxiety symptoms. These illnesses include endocrine disorders (hormone gland problems), such as thyroid disorders and problems with glucose regulation in the body, including diabetes and hypoglycemia (low blood sugar episodes).

Chronic stress syndromes and illnesses such as Chronic Fatigue Syndrome, Fibromyalgia and sleep disorders can also contribute to the symptoms of anxiety disorders

The Everything Anxiety-Coping Book!

The same is true of other pain-related illnesses such as chronic arthritis and neurological diseases as well.

Manifestations of Anxiety

Anxiety is a natural emotion but becomes a problem when it occurs too often or out-of-context, meaning it occurs at inappropriate times and is disproportionately elevated in response to insignificant triggers (phobias) or to things that should not trigger anxiety reactions. Something as simple as standing in a check-out line at a store for example should not trigger a severe anxiety reaction but can be a very real problem to people with anxiety disorders.

A perceived threat of any kind can cause some anxiety sufferers to experience panic reactions or chronic worry. They may also feel on-edge and experience apprehension about a number of things that people with normal anxiety levels give very little consideration to.

The Everything Anxiety-Coping Book!

Some anxiety disorders manifest with obsessive and/or compulsive behaviors and many anxiety sufferers exhibit the aspects or symptoms of more than one anxiety condition. If these type reactions occur for a six month period or longer, this would indicate a person is experiencing at least one anxiety disorder according to the U.S.-NIMH.

Substance Abuse and Coping Behaviors

Anxiety study groups and medical sources, including the NIMH state that anxiety disorders are often related to substance abuse and negative behaviors. Alcohol and drug abuse is often resorted-to as a coping method for chronic anxiety or in some cases the substance abuse may be a cause of anxiety conditions. Other self-coping methods some anxiety sufferers may resort to are sexually deviant behaviors and other habits of escapism, such as gambling, pornography or self-injury.

Anxiety Treatments

When anxiety disorders are related to physical illnesses, treatment for the medical condition can relieve or in some cases completely resolve the anxiety symptoms. For some medical patients, the anxiety has become a learned-behavior and may still require mental health therapy or psychotherapeutic medications (anti-anxiety drugs and/or anti-depressants). Therapies that are used to help people with anxiety disorders are designed to help them cope with anxiety and to work better with the emotion for more positive responses to it. Some therapies include "exposure techniques" in which an anxiety sufferer is slowly exposed to the phobia(s) that are causing them problems in life, so that they become less fearful of them.

Biofeedback techniques may also be used, which helps anxiety sufferers to observe their bodily responses to anxiety and stress and to develop strategies for redirecting those responses.

The Everything Anxiety-Coping Book!

This lends toward coping skills for channeling them into positive, rather than negative reactions. One of the more successful therapies is called Cognitive Behavioral Therapy which incorporates aspects of these other therapies into techniques that also help anxiety sufferers to react differently to anxiety triggers and to learn not to fear anxiety symptoms but rather to recognize them as natural bodily responses.

There will be treatment options mentioned and repeated in most chapters of this book, the reason being that some anxiety disorders or particular symptom manifestations can require slightly different treatments or different combinations of them. Treatments are generally the same however in most cases.

<u>Chapter 2.</u>

Understanding the Fight or Flight Response

The All-Important Anxiety Mechanism

Anxiety is a natural emotion, designed to inspire and protect those who experience it. Anxiety sufferers can learn to appreciate the anxiety "fight or flight response".

One important aspect for anxiety sufferers in learning to better cope with their anxiety symptoms is becoming better educated about anxiety and its intended purpose. Learning about anxiety is often a part of therapies that can successfully treat anxiety disorders by helping patients experiencing them, to better understand the purpose for the anxiety mechanism called the "fight or flight response".

Once an anxiety sufferer can view anxiety from the proper perspective, he can better learn to work with the emotion rather than fearing and avoiding it.

Anxiety is a Performance Enhancer

One of the important purposes of anxiety is to empower people to perform important tasks better and with more energy and inspiration. If a successful salesman is called upon to meet with a group of people who are seeking to achieve successful sales, he can better relate positive points for inspiring them, with the aid of the fight or flight response. An inspirational speaker is far more convincing when those listening to his lectures can see energy behind the points he is making in his speech. The same can be said of an athlete that competes for first place in a sports event. The fight or flight response can give him or her, the edge needed and the drive to reach deep down and find that extra energy at just the right moment to win the event.

In cases like these, the person experiencing this important anxiety mechanism has learned to channel the energy it provides, toward a positive outcome. Those who struggle with the fight or flight response because they tend to react negatively to it, may instead stutter and stammer when making a speech or freeze with fear when the moment of opportunity to win a sports event is facing them. This demonstrates the fact that the fight or flight response can have either a positive or negative effect, depending on how a person has learned to work with it and channel it toward positive results.

Anxiety Fight or Flight Hormones

The term "fight or flight" is reference to the fact that we may at times be faced with dangers or threats that will require us to respond by either fleeing or defending ourselves. This anxiety response enables us to do so, with added energy, alertness and strength, so that we can escape without injury or at least minimize injury when possible.

The Everything Anxiety-Coping Book!

This is accomplished by the adrenal glands that respond to danger signals from the brain and provide increased levels of adrenal hormones, the main one being "adrenaline".

Once the level of adrenaline rises, breathing increases, as well as blood flow to the muscles. The body will begin to sweat which according to anxiety research, may be the body's way of creating more difficulty in being grasped and held by an intruder, due to the skin becoming slippery with moisture. All of these bodily responses are designed to protect us but danger signals may at times be sent to the adrenal glands, from the brain, when no actual danger is present, such as when viewing a movie thriller or riding a scary amusement park ride.

The Natural Response can have an Unnatural Timing

Anxiety disorder sufferers can learn to recognize the fight or flight response as a good thing designed to empower them and protect them at the appropriate times. Anxiety that becomes "disordered" means it begins to trigger at times it is not actually needed. It may then be perceived as very unpleasant because increased energy levels are becoming available when they are not needed. Not being able to channel the fight or flight symptoms in a positive direction will cause a person to perceive them as fear rather than strength or as panic feelings, rather than the ambition needed to accomplish a task at hand.

For some anxiety sufferers, there is a subtle but chronically activated fight or flight mode that remains in a triggered state or what might be referred to as "free floating anxiety". Others have suddenly escalated fight or flight responses that are referred to as "panic attacks".

The Everything Anxiety-Coping Book!

The anxiety response itself is not unnatural but the timing of it has become disordered in these cases.

Anxiety Therapies and Treatments

There are therapies available, including a highly successful type called "Cognitive Behavioral Therapy" that helps anxiety sufferers to perceive anxiety in the correct way and to also respond to it appropriately. It also helps them learn not to fear the anxiety fight or flight response and to develop techniques for channeling it into positive outcomes rather than negative ones.

There are also medications that can aid in anxiety coping that are available in as-needed doses or that are taken as a daily regimen. These can also be combined with other anxiety therapies to increase the benefit and in some cases may only be needed temporarily as a patient better learns to cope with anxiety symptoms.

Chapter 3.

Medical Causes of Anxiety Symptoms

Health Disorders and the Fight or Flight Response

Medical research has shown that a significant percent of anxiety disorders, have underlying medical and/or endocrine gland conditions as the cause of them.

Anxiety symptoms occur due to the "fight of flight response" being triggered in the body. This anxiety mechanism, results in the release of adrenaline from the adrenal glands, so that the body can respond to an important or threatening issue that has arisen. In the case of medical conditions, the body is in some cases attempting to compensate for an abnormal change in hormone levels.

The Endocrine System

The "endocrine glands" are those in the body that supply needed hormones. These include sex hormones, adrenal hormones, thyroid hormones, the glucose regulating hormones and the master brain-gland hormones. Following is a list of some of those hormones.

• insulin - from the pancreas

• T4 and T3 – from the thyroid gland

• testosterone and estrogen - from precursor hormones (following a conversion process)

• adrenaline, cortisol, pregnenolone and DHEA – from the adrenal glands

• TSH, CRH and ACTH – from the pituitary and hypothalamus glands

The Everything Anxiety-Coping Book!

The endocrine system works in a loop, meaning the hormones are all interconnected so that they work in sync with each other, to help keep them in balance within the body. If one hormone becomes abnormally low, this can result in another hormone rising to abnormally high levels, which in some cases can result in chronic anxiety symptoms.

Thyroid Imbalance

When the body becomes low on either or both of the major thyroid hormones (T4 and T3), the thyroid-regulating "pituitary gland" in the brain sends more TSH (thyroid stimulating hormone) to the thyroid gland to prompt it to increase its production of hormones. This is a description of "hypothyroidism," meaning an under-active gland.

The opposite condition is called "hyperthyroidism" (overactive) and this is caused in many cases by too much TSH being sent to the thyroid gland. When thyroid hormone levels reach higher than normal values, hyperthyroid symptoms will result from a sped-up bodily metabolism. The resulting symptoms for this and other medical conditions that include anxiety as part of the symptom-complex may include the following:

• increased breathing (hyperventilation)

• increased heart rate (tachycardia)

• trembling (tremors)

• sudden fear (panic)

• increased body excretions (sweating, frequent urination and diarrhea)

The Everything Anxiety-Coping Book!

Hypoglycemia

When sugar enters the body via the diet, the pancreas sends out the hormone "insulin" to regulate the energy produced for the body by this very necessary fuel also called "glucose." In blood-glucose imbalance conditions, such as diabetes and reactive-hypoglycemia, the levels will drop to abnormally low levels due to insulin resistance or due to a rapid insulin reaction.

The adrenal glands will then attempt to compensate for the drop in glucose by sending out more of the hormone – adrenaline. It does this to prompt the body to produce more insulin and to replace low energy levels in the body due to low glucose levels. As this occurs, anxiety and symptoms of nervousness can result.

Mitral Valve Prolapse

This common heart murmur, abbreviated "MVP" does not cause symptoms in many people who have it, while others experience anxiety and panic symptoms frequently with the condition. Medical research studies of MVP have found that the "mitral leaflets" that support this heart valve, may become stretched-out or thickened over time and this causes the valve not to close properly with heartbeats, resulting in a "click murmur" (sound heard with a stethoscope).

The heart has many nerve impulses triggered within it that regulate the speed of heart function by interacting with the adrenal glands. With MVP, it is believed that these nerve impulses become irregular so that false signals indicating the need for increased heart rate reach the adrenal glands, causing excessive release of hormone (adrenaline surges).

This may be why panic attacks and anxiety symptoms are experienced commonly by MVP patients. One medical term for nervous system imbalance is "dysautonomia" and some medical sources refer to the condition when it is combined with nervous system imbalance as "MVP-Dysautonomia".

There are other medical conditions, in addition to the preceding three that have been described, that also cause chronic and/or sudden onset anxiety symptoms. A person, who experiences severe anxiety or panic, should see a licensed medical practitioner for definitive diagnoses of anxiety disorder or medically induced anxiety.

Chapter 4.

Anxiety Disorder Symptom Phenomena

Manifestations of Chronic Anxiety

In addition to the typical symptoms, those with anxiety disorders can also develop symptoms that further affect their thought processes and perceptions.

Anxiety disorders carry an array of symptoms including feelings of panic, hyperventilation, excessive sweating, blushing, accelerated breathing, rapid heart rate and increased blood pressure. There are other symptoms however, that specifically affect the anxiety sufferer's thinking and perception that might be termed "anxiety symptom phenomena".

Catastrophic Thinking

People experiencing anxiety disorders, may find their selves experiencing repeated concerning thoughts about the possibilities of tragic events happening to them. This may include thoughts about having violence perpetrated upon them or that they might suddenly snap and perpetrate violence upon others. They may also have chronic worries about developing life threatening or debilitating illnesses or about being involved in accidents that would cause them serious injury. Fear of failure can also plague the thoughts of anxiety sufferers as well as fear of extreme embarrassment or of looking foolish to others.

While these type thoughts affect the general population to an extent, they affect people with anxiety disorders to an exaggerated extent or what we might term "catastrophic thinking".

All anxiety disorders have potential for this type thinking to evolve in people experiencing them but more commonly among those who suffer Panic Disorder, Social Phobia and Generalized Anxiety Disorder.

Depersonalization

This symptom-phenomena, comes under the heading of an "unreality symptom" that is relatively common to chronic anxiety sufferers. It is a sensation that is experienced, that causes a person to feel less-real or that he has become unreal to self and others. While this may sound similar to delusional thinking that can occur in people with actual psychosis, it is actually a feeling and not a belief by the anxiety sufferer that he has become unreal. It is related to anxiety which is a neurosis and does not indicate the development of a psychotic disorder, although it is extremely unpleasant to those who experience it.

Some anxiety information sources state that this phenomenon is part of the "fight or flight response", the anxiety mechanism that causes focus in thinking to divert from one's self, so that any potential danger can be located and responded-to.

De-realization

This symptom-phenomena, is similar to depersonalization but this aspect of unreality symptom causes a sensation or feeling that one's surroundings have become unreal. The anxiety sufferer feels as if what he sees or experiences around him is not actually taking place but is a dream-like experience. This symptom is also very concerning and may also cause difficulty in concentrating or what might be termed "brain fog".

As with depersonalization, this too is likely a mechanism related to the fight or flight response that keeps the mind from being distracted by things that are not a danger, so that any potential dangers can be better focused on and reacted to.

Anxiety Disorder Treatments

In addition to medications such as anti-anxiety drugs and SSRI antidepressants, anxiety sufferers can learn about their disorders and learn to cope with them through "Cognitive Behavioral Therapy" (CBT) techniques. One aspect of CBT is teaching people with anxiety disorders about symptoms, what causes them and how to cope with and overcome them.

One important aspect of the therapy is also learning not to fear the symptoms and realizing that they are not harmful or dangerous and will not cause insanity or death.

Some anxiety sufferers may feel that have experienced a "nervous breakdown" however, this is not a true medical or mental health term and a more specific diagnosis can be made, with specific treatments available that can treat all types of anxiety conditions.

Chapter 5.

More about Chronic Anxiety Unreality Symptoms

Depersonalization and Derealization

For many anxiety disorder sufferers, the symptoms that are the most concerning are those that give them sensations of unreality.

These sensations referred to as "depersonalization" and "derealization," are not actual delusions or hallucinations but are rather unpleasant feelings that give the one experiencing them a feeling that reality has been altered. While this symptom-phenomenon can be very unpleasant, it does not indicate psychosis or the onset of developing insanity. These type anxiety symptoms are experienced commonly and in the vast majority of cases, are neither harmful nor dangerous.

The Everything Anxiety-Coping Book!

The Anxiety Mechanism

Anxiety researchers believe that unreality symptoms occur due to the anxiety mechanism called the "fight-or-flight response." Part of its purpose is to increase a person's concentration as it is directed toward a danger or an important task at hand that requires focus and readiness for responding to.

In the process of this, the fight-or-flight response can also cause a person's self and surroundings to fall into the background so that this increased concentration on an immediate need can occur as-necessary. With anxiety "disorder," this response begins to occur at inappropriate times or with more frequency than normal, resulting in an unpleasant perception of these symptoms.

A Vicious Cycle

When sensations of unreality occur with anxiety disorders, the focus can be on the anxiety itself that begins to be perceived as a threat or danger in the body. Fearing unpleasant anxiety responses and panic attacks can begin to serve as a "trigger" for unreality symptoms or what is also referred to as a "phobia." This can become a vicious cycle when anxiety triggers more anxiety but with treatment, chronic anxiety can be significantly diminished and in some cases overcome completely.

Unreality Symptoms

Anxiety suffers vary in symptom manifestations but there are common sensations, feelings and perceptions often described by them as related to depersonalization and derealization.

These symptoms can include the following:

Depersonalization:

• feeling unreal, like a cardboard figure or a robot

• the sensation that one is watching their own actions from outside of their body

• feeling as if others are real but they are not

• lacking recognition of oneself when looking into a mirror reflection

Derealization:

• feeling as if one's surroundings have become unreal

• the sensation that things are being looked at through a veil or a fog

• feeling as if the surrounding world is a dream or hallucination

• having momentary doubts about strongly-held beliefs

As mentioned previously, these types of unreality sensations do not represent true mental illness when they are triggered by chronic anxiety (neurosis). They are better categorized as "emotional disorder related symptoms" and a fact stated by many reputable psychiatric professionals and mental health research groups.

When true psychosis develops, a person is typically not aware of it and often, it does not present a concern to them. With anxiety disorder sufferers, it is just the opposite and they are finely tuned-in to all of their emotional and physical sensations.

Treatments

To treat unreality symptoms, the underlying anxiety disorder must be treated. All of the different types of anxiety disorders have potential to cause depersonalization and/or derealization. Cognitive Behavioral Therapy has proven to be highly successful in the treatment of anxiety disorders and symptoms. Exposure therapies, meaning those that help anxiety sufferers to slowly overcome phobias that trigger anxiety responses by gradually increasing their exposure to them has also proven to be a successful treatment.

Anti-anxiety medications and antidepressants can also benefit patients with anxiety disorders and some patients are treated with a combination of psychiatric therapy and medication. It is important that a person suffering anxiety and/or unreality type symptoms see their doctor for thorough evaluation and referral to proper treatment(s).

Chapter 6.

Obsessive-Compulsive Disorder - Basic Facts

The Anxiety Condition of Ritualistic Behaviors

According to the National Institute of Mental Health in the U.S., obsessive-compulsive disorder (OCD) affects an estimated 2.2 million adults 18 years of age and older.

OCD often begins to develop in childhood according to the NIMH and is characterized by compulsive behaviors that are driven by obsessive thoughts or worries. In most cases, these concerns are exaggerated or irrational, but this does not diminish the effect this disorder can have on the daily lives of OCD patients.

Compulsive Behaviors

The behaviors or "acting out" aspect of OCD ranges between each individual suffering the disorder. For some, they develop an intense compulsion to recheck actions they have performed to make sure they were completed thoroughly and completely. Many sufferers become perfectionists in many things they do and harshly criticize themselves if they fail to complete a task to perfection.

People with OCD will often perform the same tasks repeatedly, until they feel they have completed them at a perfect level and only then will they allow their self to move forward.

These may include:

• Not repeating an imperfect task until they are satisfied with their performance, which can cause them feelings of inward conflict resulting in severe anxiety symptoms or panic attacks?

• Repeating simple tasks such as turning off light switches or water faucets fueled by obsessive worry that they were not turned off completely.

• Unreasonable expectations of perfection for complicated tasks such as how they complete a college term paper, to avoid harsh self-criticism if they do not obtain a perfect score.

Phobias

Some OCD patients become phobic about things that concern them, such as contracting illnesses due to exposure to germs or being judged negatively if their home is not immaculately clean. This can develop into avoidance behaviors similar to those listed, following.

• Not shaking hands with people or showing other physical affections toward loved ones or friends.

• Feeling that their home is not perfectly-presentable for a visitor to see and not allowing anyone to enter their homes unless they feel the timing is perfect for doing so.

• Believing something terrible might occur to them if they do not have food arranged a certain way on their plate or if the fringes on a rug in their living room are not all laying flat and straight on the floor.

The Everything Anxiety-Coping Book!

While these types of compulsive behaviors are often seen as humorous on television shows, they can cause OCD patients to agonize and to develop chronic worries, causing them a diminished quality of life.

Frustrations

Another aspect of OCD is chronic frustration that can develop in OCD patients in the area of their communications when socializing with others. Patients with the disorder often feel they are not expressing themselves adequately. They feel the words they speak to others are not getting their thoughts across and they may begin to repeat phrases or words.

OCD patients may begin to replay conversations they've had with others repeatedly in their minds and will harshly criticize themselves for not having made certain statements or for not having worded their conversation differently.

This can also result in avoidance behaviors and when this aspect or others (as described previously) become severe, patients may become fearful of leaving their homes, a development which is known as "agoraphobia."

Treatments

Anti-anxiety and antidepressant medications are often administered to OCD patients to help reduce their symptoms. For most, however, they also require psychiatric therapy, such as Cognitive Behavioral Therapy (CBT). These type therapies are designed to help patients with OCD to change their thought patterns over time and to respond to the urge to entertain obsessive thoughts with replacement thoughts that will divert them into a positive direction.

Exposure therapy may also become a part of the treatment, in which OCD patients are slowly but repeatedly exposed to things that have become phobias or compulsions to them, so that they can better cope and possibly overcome them over time.

Chapter 7.

Post Traumatic Stress Disorder Basic Facts

Anxiety Resulting From Chronic Stressors or Trauma

The U.S. National Institute of Mental Health (NIMH) places Post Traumatic Stress Disorder (PTSD) as the second most common anxiety condition, second to social phobia.

The NIHM statistics for the U.S. reveal that approximately 7.7 million Americans are experiencing the disorder and many more people worldwide. The majority of sufferers are adults, with the most common age of onset being people in their early 20s.

Who Experiences PTSD?

PTSD is a common anxiety disorder partly due to the fact that it affects millions of war veterans who have developed this condition of chronic stress during wartime, following combat duties. In the early days of its recognition in soldiers, it was referred to by names such as "combat fatigue" and "soldier's heart."

It can also result from other traumatic experiences, including accidents that result in serious physical injuries to one's self or from witnessing or causing accidents in which death or injury occurs to loved ones or to anyone who is terminally injured.

PTSD can also result in those who have had violent and/or sexually deviant behaviors perpetrated upon them and in those whose loved ones have suddenly passed away or have departed from them under difficult

The Everything Anxiety-Coping Book!

circumstances (sometimes referred to as "separation anxiety" in these cases).

Symptoms of PTSD

As with other anxiety disorders, PTSD causes frequent triggering of the "fight or flight response", the anxiety mechanism that increases adrenaline in the body. The resulting symptoms can include panic attacks and free-floating type anxiety symptoms in which a person feels continually anxious, apprehensive and on-edge.

Some of the characteristic symptoms that set PTSD apart from other anxiety disorders include nightmares involving the traumatic event(s) experienced by the disorder sufferer and flashbacks in which they believe they are reliving the events that triggered the disorder. While flashbacks are a type of delusion, this does not place PTSD in the "psychosis" category, but it is still considered to be a condition of "neurosis."

Treatments

The more common type of medication therapy used to treat PTSD patients is SSRI antidepressants. However, this type of anxiety disorder usually requires psychiatric therapy for patients to successfully cope with the disorder and for possible resolution of it (complete recovery). Cognitive Behavioral Therapy has been found to be highly successful in helping patients recover from this and other chronic anxiety disorders.

Other therapies that may be administered, in combination with drug treatment or as single treatments, include therapies called "Eye Movement Desensitization and Reprocessing" (EMDR), "Exposure Therapy" (facing the event mentally to find closure) and aspects of therapy that help sexually traumatized victims realize they are not at fault and should not be experiencing guilt over their experiences.

Anyone who believes they may be experiencing symptoms of PTSD should see their medical doctor or a licensed mental health professional as soon as possible.

Chapter 8.

Panic Disorder Basic Information

The Condition of Chronic Climaxed Anxiety Attacks

Of all the anxiety disorders that affect millions of people worldwide, panic disorder is arguably the most unpleasant and concerning one that is experienced.

The vast majority of people in the general population have experienced a panic attack at some point in their lives. For some the attack was triggered by a sudden fear-provoking event, a sudden trauma or by something that caused them an intense thrill.

For others who experience panic attacks however, they begin to trigger for inappropriate reasons and more frequently than normal.

The Everything Anxiety-Coping Book!

When this occurs, the condition has become a panic disorder and may continue to worsen if the sufferer does not seek treatment. About 6-million people in the U.S. alone suffer from panic disorder according to the NIMH.

Panic Attack Symptoms

Anxiety symptoms in general include feelings of fear, sped-up heart rate and breathing, tightness in the chest, tensed muscles, lightheadedness, diverted concentration, profuse sweating, body tremors, intense blushing and dry mouth. With panic attacks, these symptoms occur suddenly and with strong intensity and if they occur with frequency, the term "panic disorder" would apply.

Panic can also cause feelings of unreality referred to as "depersonalization and derealization" and those suffering them often experience catastrophic thoughts, such as believing the attacks will cause them heart attacks, insanity or sudden death.

Panic Disorder Restricts Lives

In the vast majority of people who suffer panic disorder, the condition doesn't pose a serious threat to health and with anxiety being a condition of "neurosis" and not "psychosis", the fear of insanity it may cause is an irrational thought and will not occur. This does not take away from the fact that these type fears often accompany the disorder and as a result can cause sufferers to begin avoiding things they fear may trigger panic attacks (phobias).

Triggers for panic can begin to increase over time, so that many different things become phobias to a panic disorder patient.

The Everything Anxiety-Coping Book!

Something as simple as shopping at a supermarket can cause panic attacks in susceptible individuals because they feel they are in a situation where an attack will cause them embarrassment and that they will find it hard to escape without notice from others. They may feel trapped in a sense in any place where they feel panic may occur or where it might be difficult for them to receive emergency care.

Panic That Develops into Agoraphobia

Some people with panic episodes commonly experience thoughts of needing to be taken to hospital emergency rooms and some do actually check into emergency rooms when experiencing their first attack(s). When panic disorder causes severe restriction of activities a patient may also be diagnosed with "agoraphobia", another anxiety condition in which a person becomes fearful to venture outside of their home. This is why it is important that treatment is administered as early as possible in people who develop a panic disorder.

The Everything Anxiety-Coping Book!

Treatments

Panic disorder is responsive to medications commonly used to treat anxiety symptoms, such as Selective Serotonin Reuptake Inhibitors (SSRIs), Tricyclic Antidepressants (TCAs), Monoamine OxidaseInhibitors (MAOIs) and Benzodiazepines.

Natural supplements that are reported to be helpful to some anxiety sufferers who use them include Valerian, Kava and Chamomile teas, St. John's Wort, Gamma-Aminobutyric Acid (GABA) and SAMe(S-Adenosyl-Methionine). Herbals and natural supplements should however be approved by your doctor especially if you are treated with prescription medications of any kind.

Psychiatric therapies can also be effective in treating anxiety disorders and in helping anxiety patients learn coping methods including those who suffer panic attacks.

The Everything Anxiety-Coping Book!

Cognitive Behavioral Therapy (CBT) continues to be one of the more successful therapies available with a high treatment success rate.

Treatment options should be discussed with a licensed doctor or mental health care professional.

Chapter 9.

Generalized Anxiety Disorder Basic Facts

The Condition of Chronic Worry

Nearly 7-million adults suffer from Generalized Anxiety Disorder (GAD) in the U.S. alone and for some this chronic anxiety condition can become disabling.

It is not unusual or abnormal to have worries in life about problems regarding family, employment, school and health to a reasonable degree but when worry crosses over the line and becomes obsessive and chronic, it becomes an anxiety disorder. GAD is the term for this type of anxiety but treatments are available for those who are diagnosed with it.

Symptoms and Manifestations of GAD

People, who experience GAD, will have chronic excessive worry for at least six months, to meet the diagnostic criteria as described by the U.S. National Institute of Mental Health. The worry will often keep them from getting proper rest and sleep, due to the continued troubling or racing thoughts that they find very difficult not to entertain and to ponder repeatedly in their minds. People with GAD often feel they are experiencing a nervous breakdown.

GAD patients often worry about things such as contracting a terminal illness or that it might happen to one of their loved ones or that a tragic event will strike their family. They may also worry about losing their job or that their spouse will leave them when there is no rational reason for these concerns to occur.

They may also obsess over the possibility of being a failure at their job or other pursuits in life that are important to them.

The Everything Anxiety-Coping Book!

They often feel on-edge and very apprehensive in these areas and this will often cause avoidance behaviors, meaning they resist attempting to succeed at new endeavors of self-improvement for fear of failure or disappointment.

Patients with GAD often feel highly stressed (stressed-out) due to the many things they continually worry about. This can contribute to feelings of low mood and depression, which commonly co-exist with GAD. Panic attacks may also occur in some patients with this anxiety disorder, as can elements of Obsessive Compulsive Disorder (OCD).

Some GAD Patients are Over-Achievers

Another aspect of this anxiety disorder can be obsessive thoughts in the area of self-achievements. People with GAD may constantly feel they have not achieved enough success in life and as a result they will push their selves toward unreasonable goals.

The Everything Anxiety-Coping Book!

They will fall into this behavior pattern, rather than allowing achievements to occur at a reasonable pace for them. This can create a vicious cycle of added stressors, followed by disappointments over not achieving the unreasonable goals they set for themselves.

People with Gad may also multi-task to an unreasonable degree due to their worry that duties and obligations will mount and become overwhelming to them. They become obsessed with staying ahead of their tasks, to the point that they cause added stress and become sensitized to anxiety rather than achieving the stress-relief they are seeking. Some people, who appear to be "work-a-alcoholics", may actually be suffering from GAD.

Treatments for GAD

Medications, including anti-anxiety drugs and anti-depressants are often prescribed to help reduce the symptoms of GAD.

The Everything Anxiety-Coping Book!

These may include selective serotonin reuptake inhibitors (SSRI-a type of anti-depressant) which, comes in brands such as Paxil, Prozac and Zoloft. Some patients may also be prescribed benzodiazepines (anxiety drugs) that help to offer immediate relief of anxiety symptoms as-needed which comes in brands such as Xanax, Kolonopin, and Adavan.

Psychiatric therapies such as Cognitive Behavioral Therapy (CBT) can also help a great deal in gaining patients coping skills or the ability to overcome their anxiety disorders completely over time. Some prescribed treatments may include a combination of therapy and anxiety-reducing medications.

Chapter 10.

Social Anxiety Disorder Basic Facts

When Socializing is Terrifying

When a person experiences intense anxiety reactions to social settings and events, they are suffering from social phobia also called "Social Anxiety Disorder".

The U.S. National Institute of Mental Health (NIMH) states that approximately 15 million adult Americans and many, more worldwide experience Social Anxiety Disorder (SAD). This places it as the single most common chronic anxiety condition that exists. The disorder affects from people from all walks of life and in recent years, entertainer Donny Osmond came forward to announce that he has struggled with SAD since childhood.

Social Phobia Goes Beyond Shyness

Most people experience a degree of shyness when meeting new people or even those they are already acquainted with socially. With SAD, the shyness is extreme and exaggerated, causing the sufferer to feel very uneasy, on-edge or even panicky when he is in a social setting. The typical symptoms of anxiety will manifest when SAD sufferers are in the presence of people they are uncomfortable with, which is usually everyone outside of their immediate family and very close friends.

SAD Symptoms

The symptoms of anxiety experienced by people with SAD include the common ones which are feelings of panic and apprehension, trembling, an urge to escape, rapid heart rate and breathing, muscle tension, feelings of unreality (depersonalization and derealization) and dizziness.

The Everything Anxiety-Coping Book!

The anxiety symptoms that seem to be more intense in SAD sufferers are feelings of embarrassment, blushing, dry mouth, sweating and feeling that others are judging them. Symptoms can vary among those with SAD, depending on how developed the disorder is. Some will experience symptoms even while meeting with only one person, while symptoms only manifest in others when they are in social settings with several people present.

Inappropriate Timing of the Fight or Flight Response

Research studies by mental health groups in regard to social phobia have found that most patients develop the disorder during childhood. Over time, learned behaviors develop that cause the "fight of flight response" to become triggered more often and at inappropriate times, when SAD sufferers attempt to be active socially. The anxiety itself is not an unnatural emotion but it is the timing of it that becomes disordered (not in the order intended).

The Everything Anxiety-Coping Book!

Socially phobic people have learned to recognize social events and meeting new people, as a threat to them.

Treatments for SAD

There are psychiatric therapies including those in the "Cognitive Behavioral Therapy" category that help people with SAD, to change the way they think about social events and settings. They also learn to respond differently to the feelings and symptoms of anxiety, so that they can channel the energy produced by it into putting their best foot forward when meeting new people. It is a therapy that helps anxiety patients to react positively to anxiety, so that it works for them, rather than against them.

There are also medications that can be combined with psychiatric therapies when needed or taken as a single treatment, including anti-anxiety drugs and SSRI anti-depressants.

The Everything Anxiety-Coping Book!

People with SAD should also self-educate about their disorder because knowledge can become power to help them overcome SAD or to greatly diminish the effects of it (coping) in their lives.

Chapter 11.

Anxiety Disorders and Catastrophic Thinking

Chronic Thoughts of Irrational Worry

Catastrophic thinking is an area of chronic anxiety symptomology, in which people suffering anxiety disorders experience ongoing irrational thoughts.

While this type of thinking occurs commonly with anxiety disorders, these unpleasant thoughts that might be termed as the "what-ifs" seldom have a basis of reality to them and are not acted upon by most anxiety disorder sufferers.

The anxiety disorder that most often involves entertaining thoughts of chronic worry is "Generalized Anxiety Disorder" but the worries can also be about everyday events in addition to fears of catastrophic ones (phobic thinking).

The Everything Anxiety-Coping Book!

When worries become more than entertained thoughts and are frequently acted upon, the anxiety disorder would then likely be classified as "Obsessive Compulsive Disorder". All anxiety disorders have potential to produce catastrophic thinking, including Post Traumatic Stress, Social and Panic disorders.

What is Catastrophic Thinking?

This area of irrational thinking involves thoughts by the anxiety sufferer, of impending doom or of a danger he believes threatens him, a terminal disease he is about to experience, and fears of losing control or of becoming violent to others. Examples of these types of thoughts would include the fear of harming one's own child or family members or the fear that every new mole, freckle or bump found on one's body indicates developing cancer. Similar areas of chronic worry may include thoughts that one will be involved in a traumatic accident or will experience a negative life-changing event at any moment.

This type of thinking is common to chronic anxiety sufferers and has aspects to it that are similar to Obsessive Compulsive Disorder as mentioned previously, with exception of the fact that the what-if thoughts remain as highly concerning worries that are not acted upon by the anxiety disorder sufferer. There are however some anxiety patients who experience aspects and symptom-manifestations of more than one anxiety disorder at a time and in these cases, catastrophic thinking may be accompanied by compulsive behaviors.

The Fight or Flight Response

Information sources that provide education on anxiety disorders and symptoms, state that catastrophic thinking is triggered by the "fight or flight response" which is the anxiety mechanism that places the mind and body in a protective or reactive state. If for example, a person finds himself in actual danger that is real and not imagined, the fight or flight response provides added energy to respond to that threat.

The Everything Anxiety-Coping Book!

If a vicious dog runs toward him, as he walks down the sidewalk to pick up the morning newspaper, the anxiety mechanism supplies a surge of adrenaline for bolting toward the front door of the house to enter a place of safety.

Perceived Dangers

With catastrophic thinking, a person is not in real danger even though the fight or flight response is activating and so her mind begins to scan for all possible dangers that might threaten her. This causes the mind to venture into the area of possible events that have very little chance of happening but despite this fact, the thoughts are frightening and very concerning to those who experience them. Even the anxiety sufferer often recognizes the thoughts as being irrational but will find it very difficult to keep them from occurring repeatedly.

This could also be referred to as "phobic thinking" and with anxiety disorders a person inadvertently trains her mind to develop fears of perceived dangers.

Treatments

The fact that it takes a process of time for an anxiety disorder to develop also means it takes time to reverse phobic thoughts that serve as triggers for anxiety attacks. There are psychiatric therapies, self-therapies and medications that can help with catastrophic thinking and that are effective in treating underlying anxiety disorders in-general.

Cognitive Behavioral Therapy (CBT) and other types of therapies that help retrain the mind can effectively treat catastrophic thought patterns by helping anxiety patients recognize this type thinking as being irrational so that they respond to it differently.

They can also learn techniques that help them not to entertain these type thoughts and to recognize the fact that when they do occur, it does not indicate the onset of insanity.

Self-therapy techniques can also help anxiety sufferers to divert their thoughts away from irrational worry and catastrophic thinking. Keeping one's mind occupied with art, writing, hobbies and self-improvement pursuits can be helpful in this area. Also using humor as a diversion technique can be effective by finding ways to laugh at irrational thoughts rather than adding more fear to them.

Psychiatric medications that treat anxiety symptoms on an as-needed basis or ones that are taken on a daily basis to control symptoms can be effective when added to other therapies as well.

These include benzodiazepines, SSRI antidepressants, Tricyclic Antidepressants, Monoamine Oxidase Inhibitors and Azapirones. A treating doctor or mental health professional can determine via discussion with anxiety patients, which medication is best suited for them.

Chapter 12

More about Methods for Coping with Panic Attacks

Dealing with a Climax of Anxiety Symptoms

Panic attacks can occur independently or as feature of other anxiety disorders. There are methods that help diminish symptoms or to possibly overcome panic episodes.

According to statistics published by the U.S. National Institutes of Mental Health (NIMH) approximately 6 million adult Americans suffer panic attacks, most of them experiencing their first episode in early adulthood. About one-third of panic disorder (frequent occurrence) sufferers will also develop "agoraphobia" meaning they will have significant restrictions in their ability to venture from their homes and to carry on with daily obligations. Some cases of panic disorder can be related to physical illnesses.

The Everything Anxiety-Coping Book!

Panic Attack Symptoms

These escalated episodes of anxiety symptoms might be referred to as a "climax of anxiety" because of the sudden and powerful manifestation of them. The symptoms of panic include severe fear reactions, increases in breathing and heart rate, the need to go to the bathroom (increased urination and bowel movements), profuse sweating and muscle tension and an urge to escape. Some people who suffer panic attacks also experience unreality type symptoms, referred to as derealization and depersonalization which cause self and/or surroundings to feel unreal and foggy. Panic sufferers often fear they will lose control, suffer a heart attack, experience sudden death or lose their sanity.

Triggers for Panic

Another term for a phobia that can set off panic symptoms can also be referred to as a "trigger" that causes the episodes.

The Everything Anxiety-Coping Book!

These can be different for each person but some examples of triggers would be things like being in a crowd of people, feeling trapped in a dentist chair, being called upon to speak in front of an audience, seeing an animal or insect a person fears or even something as simple as standing in line at a department store check-out stand. All anxiety disorders can have panic attacks associated with them and chronic stress or trauma that leads to feeling overwhelmed may become triggers as well. The triggered anxiety mechanism is called the "fight or flight response".

Self Education an Important Anxiety Therapy

One important aspect in gaining coping abilities and in possibly overcoming panic symptoms completely is for panic sufferers to learn about their anxiety condition.

This type of self-education helps them to see anxiety as a natural emotion, designed as a safety feature to help them escape from or protect their selves from real dangers or to perform tasks that require additional inspiration and energy.

Patients with chronic anxiety can begin to recognize their anxiety as something meant to help them, rather than hinder them and may lend toward an ability to work better with the emotion in positive ways rather than suffering negative effects from it.

Panic Treatments

Other therapies that include self-education as previously described include Cognitive Behavioral Therapy, Exposure Therapy, Breathing and Muscle Relaxation Techniques, exercise and meditation. Diet improvements can also help by eliminating refined sugars (candy, pie, cake, cookies and soft drinks) which can cause blood-sugar (glucose) to also drop adversely or what is referred to as "hypoglycemia". Replacing these unhealthy foods with healthy ones and eliminating stimulants that can contribute to anxiety can be helpful as well. Stimulants that can aggravate anxiety symptoms include caffeine, alcohol and tobacco products.

Prescription and Natural Anti-Anxiety Drugs and Remedies

Prescription as-needed anti-anxiety medications can also help such as Xanax, Ativan and Klonopin if a treating doctor determines a patient needs them. Daily regimen medications may also be prescribed that require daily dosing, including Paxil, Prozac, Lexapro and Zoloft. Natural over-the-counter anxiety-reducing remedies include Valerian extract, Panicyl, St. John's Wort, Passion Flower, Bach's Rescue Remedy and SAMe.

Any natural supplements should be taken at the manufacturer's suggested dose and should be approved by a doctor as a precaution against any adverse risks they might pose if they are not compatible with other treatments a patient is undergoing.

Chapter 13.

Is Nervous Breakdown a True Medical Term?

When the Stress of Life becomes Overwhelming

A "nervous breakdown" can mean that a person has become chronically stressed-out, is experiencing an emotional disorder or burnout. Effective treatments are available.

The term "nervous breakdown" is not recognized widely in modern medicine as a genuine illness. It is a catch-all term describing a number of mental and emotional states one may arrive at when overwhelmed with problems or stressors that one is unable to fully cope with. While the term was more widely used decades ago, medical doctors and mental health professionals are now more precise with diagnoses, so that emotional disorders and stress related syndromes can receive the specific treatments needed.

The Everything Anxiety-Coping Book!

Nervous Breakdown - a General Term of Convenience

In the past, when someone of celebrity or notoriety was experiencing personal problems and he did not want public disclosure of details regarding it, the nervous breakdown label was often placed on it. This kept him from having to reveal facts that might cause a negative perception of him that could destroy his public image or positive reputation. In some cases, problems with drug or alcohol abuse were placed under this term but it was also used to describe people who had reached a point of burn-out or who were displaying frequent fits of rage (temper tantrums).

Other times it was the term used to simply inform others that the person in question was simply exhausted and in serious need of time for rest and recovery from becoming stressed-out. Other terms used to describe these type conditions involving chronic stress were "nervous exhaustion" and "neurasthenia".

The Everything Anxiety-Coping Book!

Stress Syndromes

One of the more common stress syndromes is one referred to as "Adrenal Fatigue", a condition in which prolonged or traumatic stress (chronic) causes a diminished ability in the adrenal glands to moderate daily stressors due to low reserves of the hormone "cortisol".

A more serious stress-related syndrome is "Chronic Fatigue Syndrome" that is also often experienced due to chronic stress. Research studies of CFS have cited the fact that people who have the disorder are experiencing a "blunted" response by the endocrine glands that work in-sync to moderate stress, called the "Hypothalamus-Pituitary-Adrenal Axis".

Fibromyalgia is similar to CFS, in fact medical sources state that the two conditions have 75% crossover similarities and both are cited as being stress-related in some patients who experience them.

The Everything Anxiety-Coping Book!

Some people who are termed as having nervous breakdowns could very well be experiencing one of these stress-related syndromes.

Anxiety Disorders

Stress often leads to anxiety reactions and for some people, the anxiety mechanism called the "fight or flight response" begins to trigger frequently or at times that it should not normally be happening. When this type of frequency or bad-timing is experienced for a six month period or longer, it is referred to as "anxiety disorder" (disordered - not in the order intended).

Added stressors or those that become overwhelming can begin to serve as triggers for ongoing anxiety responses and this scenario is often referred to as "anxiety sensitization".

People who experience the onset of anxiety disorders and especially those who become agoraphobic (fear of leaving their home) or who experience panic attacks, are sometimes recognized and having nervous breakdowns.

Major Depression

Chronic stress can also lead to feelings of depression, as can major life-changes or experiences of traumatic loss in one's life. It is normal to experience depression to a reasonable degree and for normal lengths of time following stressful experiences or events of loss, such as the death of a loved-one or after being laid off from a long held job. If however, a reasonable time has transpired for grieving or to recover from the stress of an event but full recovery is not experienced, it can be an indication of major depression (Major Depressive Disorder-MDD).

This emotional/mood disorder causes a person to feel profoundly sad and to lose interest in things that once brought them pleasure or happiness. This often causes them to withdraw from others and from normal activities that no longer hold interest for them. Those who witness the onset of major depression in others may recognize it as a nervous breakdown.

Treatments

The treatment for what might be recognized as a nervous breakdown would depend on what the specific diagnosis actually reveals. If stress syndromes are the cause, supplements may be administered to boost adrenal function that has become diminished and to help patients reduce and manage stress levels. If CFS or Fibromyalgia are diagnosed, additional treatments for joint and muscle aches, sleep problems and emotional symptoms may be combined to effectively treat these syndromes as a whole.

Emotional disorders of anxiety and/or depression may require psychiatric therapies and/or drug therapies to reduce and control a patient's symptoms. Additionally, Cognitive Behavioral Therapies may be incorporated into the treatment for emotional disorders, to help patients learn to cope and to potentially overcome their disorders.

Chapter 14.

Chronic Anxiety Associated with Thyroid Disorder

Symptoms of Anxiety Induced by Thyroid Disease

An earlier chapter addressed the fact that anxiety can be medically induced by a health disorder. With anxiety disorders affecting an estimated 27-million Americans and many more worldwide, this chapter will specifically address anxiety symptoms that are related to thyroid disorders and diseases. Chronic anxiety symptoms are common in both hypothyroid and hyperthyroid conditions. The cause can be rooted in both hormone imbalance and thyroid autoimmunity.

An overactive thyroid gland or "hyperthyroidism" often causes anxiety symptoms, due to an abnormal increase of metabolism in the body.

The Everything Anxiety-Coping Book!

The thyroid sets the metabolic rate of every cell in the body via hormones produced by the gland. When the levels of hormones increase to abnormally high levels (thyrotoxicity), the metabolism becomes speeded up, causing all organs in the body to operate at overdrive, including the endocrine system (glands that release hormones). This means the body's response to burning energy sources coming into the body, including food and oxygen is over-reactive, so that these are used faster than the body normally needs them (hyper-metabolism and hyperventilation).

The rate at which the pancreas regulates glucose (blood sugar) via release of the hormone insulin is also increased as are hormones from the adrenal gland including adrenaline which sets the rate of blood pressure and heart function (pulse). The combination of all of these functions and mechanisms running abnormally high causes symptoms of increased energy, nervousness and anxiety symptoms.

People with hyperthyroidism experience a generalized increase in free-floating anxiety, a feeling of being on edge and periods of suddenly escalated anxiety called panic attacks.

Hashitoxicosis from Hashimoto's thyroiditis

Most cases of hypothyroidism in industrialized countries are caused by an autoimmune condition called "Hashimoto's thyroiditis". The under-functioning of the thyroid gland in cases of Hashimoto's, is a result of auto-antibodies that are created and released by the immune system, to attack proteins found in the thyroid gland, causing cell death and eventual damage to the gland. Once enough damage has occurred, the thyroid gland's ability to produce sufficient amounts of hormones is diminished.

"Hashitoxicosis" is an intermittent period of hyperthyroidism experienced by some patients with Hashimoto's.

As the hyperthyroid phases occur, sudden and severe anxiety symptoms may manifest, as well as other symptoms of hyperthyroidism. Types of temporary thyroiditis (sub-acute), that are non-autoimmune related that can occur in pregnant women and in people with respiratory viruses can also cause short term hyperthyroidism.

Medical research studies state that Hashitoxicosis does not have to occur for anxiety symptoms to be caused by Hashimoto's, the permanent type thyroiditis but have concluded that anxiety may be associated with the "thyroid autoimmunity" itself.

Hot Thyroid Nodules and Toxic Diffuse Goiters

Tumors may develop in the thyroid gland, called "nodules" and these can be the type that, become "hot", meaning they release thyroid hormone as if they have become part of the gland.

When these type nodules become active enough to cause hyperthyroidism, anxiety symptoms may be a part of the symptom-complex that results, as with hyperthyroidism of other causes.

In some patients, the thyroid gland becomes enlarged with or without containing thyroid nodules. This is referred to as a goiter but the gland may also become toxic (overactive) as a result of the goiter, which is referred to as a "toxic diffuse goiter". Most people with autoimmune-caused hyperthyroidism or "Graves' disease" have toxic diffuse goiters. If there is a combination of goiter and nodules, it may be referred to as a multi-nodular - toxic diffuse goiter.

Treatment for Anxiety caused by Thyroid Disorders

For most cases of anxiety symptoms related to thyroid disorders, treating the disorder itself will bring relief of symptoms or even complete resolution of them.

The Everything Anxiety-Coping Book!

In cases of autoimmune-related hypothyroidism, replacing the low hormone levels, will correct the metabolism and help to reduce or control the thyroid antibody levels. In cases of hyperthyroidism, regardless of cause, reducing thyroid hormone levels using "anti-thyroid" and/or "beta-blocker" medications will reduce or resolve symptoms in some cases.

In more severe cases of hyperthyroidism, that cannot be controlled with these type drugs partial or full thyroid removal (thyroidectomy surgery) may be necessary or destruction of the gland by radioactive iodine (ablation). Removal of part or all of the thyroid gland may also be required in cases of hot nodules and toxic diffuse goiters.

If these treatments still do not relieve anxiety symptoms, anti-anxiety medications or SSRI antidepressants may be prescribed. Therapies to help patients cope with anxiety may also be recommended, such as "Cognitive Behavioral Therapy", which has been found to be a very effective treatment for anxiety conditions.

Chapter 15.

The Symptom Phenomenon of Anxiety Sensitization

When Phobic Reactions Are Easily Triggered by Stress

Anxiety disorder sufferers can go through phases in which anxiety symptoms are more easily triggered but there are methods for helping to avoid anxiety-sensitization.

People who experience chronic anxiety can very likely relate the fact that they have periods of time in which they experience higher degrees of anxiety manifestations. Symptoms seem to occur more often or more severely when they are in this state of being sensitized to anxiety triggers.

Stress and Anxiety Symptoms

Stress is a term simply meaning there is pressure being applied to the mind and emotions. When stress levels are elevated, this is one of the most common reasons for anxiety to manifest. Anxiety in fact is a response to stress and is the body's built-in mechanism that warns us when we begin to feel we are in a state of danger, so that we remain ready to respond to it by escaping it or defending ourselves against it (fight or flight response).

Chronic stress causes feelings of being overwhelmed to build and can also cause a person to feel trapped in situations that begin to feel very unpleasant to them. This causes the anxiety mechanism to trigger because it causes a person to feel a need to escape these types of situations or to at least find relief from them.

Anxiety symptoms can include feelings of apprehension, a sense of being overwhelmed, agitation and irritability, nervousness, increased heart rate and breathing, sweating and trembling.

Fatigue and Illness

Most anxiety disorder sufferers can also relate to the fact that when they are extra tired either mentally or physically, this can cause them to experience anxiety symptoms more easily. These type things can add more stress to that already being experienced. Being involved in mental studies for long periods of time without taking breaks to unwind can also have this effect on people with anxiety. Staring at a computer screen for too long or working on tax returns for example, without taking needed-breaks can increase stress levels, causing anxiety to trigger more easily.

Coping Methods

People with anxiety disorders should learn to recognize those things that cause them added stress (stressors) and eliminate as many of them as possible, also learning to take as much stress as possible out of any remaining ones. Anxiety disorder sufferers often find it difficult to pace their selves in their performance of duties and chores that face them on a daily basis. People with "Generalized Anxiety Disorder" and "Obsessive Compulsive Disorder" for example, feel that if they don't take care of every issue immediately, their duties will build and overwhelm them at some point. This requires using methods for giving their selves permission, to take breaks and enjoy leisure activities that can reduce their stress levels.

Getting involved in exercise techniques that help the body to relax can also help, as well as relaxation methods, such as muscle-stretching and deep-breathing exercises.

The Everything Anxiety-Coping Book!

Taking time to enjoy hobbies, self improvement activities and art pursuits, such as writing, painting or sculpting can also be beneficial in reducing stress. If the added, benefit of other anxiety treatments are needed, such as anti-anxiety/anti-depressant medications and/or psychiatric therapies, these can be combined with stress-reducing practices, for added results when needed.

Chapter 16.

More about Chronic Anxiety and Panic Coping Methods

Dealing with the Fight or Flight Response

Chronic anxiety is the most common emotional disorder that exists, running close second to depressive disorders, but there are effective methods for coping.

According to Psychologist Thomas A. Richards, Ph.D., Director of The Anxiety Network International, anxiety sufferers often believe they will experience catastrophic results from anxiety symptoms. These fears are irrational, however, and the events will not occur the vast majority of the time. They are, however, very real concerns to people with chronic anxiety.

The Everything Anxiety-Coping Book!

The Fight or Flight Response

The "fight or flight response" is a reaction that results in all bodily functions increasing temporarily once stimulated by the release of the adrenal gland hormone adrenaline. The response is normally activated when there is a genuine need for it, such as during times of danger or for tasks of performance that require added inspiration, strength or ambition.

When anxiety sufferers experience the onset of unpleasant anxiety or panic symptoms that are not triggered for legitimate, normal reasons this may instead result in a sense of impending doom.

The following are some of the catastrophic fears that can result from severe anxiety and panic symptoms that do not occur with normal anxiety responses.

• fear of losing sanity

• fear of fainting

• fear of experiencing a heart attack

• fear of running out of oxygen

• fear of losing control and becoming violent or behaving bizarrely

• fear of needing an ambulance or emergency room

These types of thoughts arise in some people when the fight or flight response activates because it begins to do so at inopportune times.

The Everything Anxiety-Coping Book!

Rather than occurring when there is need for extra strength or inspiration to perform a task at hand, it will instead trigger because of specific and/or varied phobias that develop (deeply embedded fears).

For some anxiety sufferers, a phobia can be something as simple as an activity that should not normally result in anxiety responses. Anxiety can become severe in some cases and cause the sufferer to become fearful of venturing outdoors (agoraphobia).

Following are examples of phobias that can be experienced by people with anxiety disorders:

• fear of walking down shopping isles at stores

• being in a crown of people

• being called on to speak before an audience

• anticipating a panic attack regardless of where one is or what one is doing.

Self Educating

A major first step toward coping and recovery for anxiety sufferers is to become better educated about anxiety. By doing this, it can be learned that anxiety is a natural emotion designed to protect a person when in danger and to give added inspiration when one is performing an important task. These facts can be liberating and can aid toward learning methods for working with anxiety responses rather than feeling threatened by them.

Anxiety sufferers can, in essence, learn to channel anxiety into a positive energy at every opportunity as well. This area of coping takes practice and planning but can yield excellent results with time and effort.

The Everything Anxiety-Coping Book!

Diversion Techniques

Having pursuits to work on that allow creative use of the mind can also be a channel for redirecting anxiety responses into creative energy. When projects such as works of art, writing and improving in a sport or activity are being planned and worked on, a person with anxiety disorder can divert anxiety thoughts toward building these projects into final outcomes that offer a sense of accomplished and achievement. This method is sometimes referred to as a "diversion technique."

Connecting with other anxiety sufferers by joining forums for people with panic and anxiety disorders can also be greatly helpful. This helps one to gain awareness that anxiety problems are not rare but are experienced by millions of other people. It also helps one learn facts about anxiety rather than giving attention to its symptoms.

It can also be a source of therapy to share one's anxiety experiences, symptoms and gains in coping with other anxiety patients by writing them in blogs, articles or forum posts.

Finding Effective Anxiety Programs

Anxiety patients should discuss treatment options with a doctor and ask questions about all available anxiety therapies. Doctors can often refer their anxiety disorder patients to therapists and programs designed to help in coping and recovery and prescribe medications when needed. An online search can also direct people who suffer anxiety to programs offering self-help therapy including a highly successful method called "Cognitive Behavioral Therapy" (CBT).

Coping with chronic anxiety and panic attacks often comes with better results when a patient is actively involved in their treatment and in the ongoing practice of coping techniques.

Section Three: **Treatments for Medically Caused Anxiety and Depression**

<u>Chapter 1.</u>

More about Medical Causes of Anxiety

Mitral Valve Prolapse (MVP) and Mitral Valve Prolapse-Syndrome(MVPS)

This common condition that causes a "click murmur" in the heart has been studied by medical groups and found to be a common cause of anxiety symptoms and panic attacks. The irregular heartbeats caused by MVPS are due to slight abnormalities in the mitral valve leaflets, or the supporting valve chords, or both. These structures allow the leaflet(s) to prolapse (or buckle) back into the left atrium during the heart's contraction-ventricular systole.

While medical research has not concluded definitively what causes the mitral valve to prolapse abnormally in some people, they theorize that it is due to these valve leaflets becoming either thickened or stretched out over time and this causes them to vibrate or quiver slightly. This is why it is referred to as a "click murmur" due to the sound it can sometimes make when the heartbeat is listened to closely with a stethoscope. Though statistics vary in regard to the number of Americans that have this disorder, one of the more commonly published statistics states that up to 1 in 5 Americans have Mitral Valve Prolapse.

For most patients, this common disorder does not cause symptoms but for those in whom it does, it is referred to as "Mitral Valve Prolapse Syndrome" (MVPS). While there have yet to be definitive reasons found for why this usually benign heart irregularity causes these anxiety symptoms, there are several theories considered.

The most accepted theory is that small, irregular changes in electrical impulses that take place in the heart that are regulated by the involuntary nervous system cause too much release of adrenaline from the adrenal glands.

Normally adrenaline is released to change the pace of the heart's beating to compensate for increased physical activity (sympathetic response) or when there is a change in body-posture, such as standing from a seated position (postural blood pressure). With Mitral Valve Prolapse the irregular nerve impulses to the heart trigger these adrenaline surges, causing increased anxiety symptoms.

If you suspect that MVPS could be the cause of anxiety symptoms you are experiencing, the symptoms I've discussed are simply observations that should prompt a visit to your licensed physician for further evaluation. Once a patient suspecting MVP can describe their symptoms to their doctor, he can perform a physical, including listening closely to the patient's heart.

He may detect a heart murmur by stethoscope but in many cases, MVP cannot be detected unless the patient is sent/referred to a cardiologist (heart specialist) for a test called an "echo cardiogram." This test is similar to ultrasound in that it uses very sensitive sound waves, transmitted onto a screen, so that the function of the heart can be monitored very clearly. If a patient has Mitral Valve Prolapse, the condition will be detected and definitively diagnosed using this diagnostic test.

Treatment for anxiety and other symptoms of MVP may include beta-blocker medications that help control the effects of adrenaline in the body and/or anti-anxiety and antidepressant medications.

More severe cases of MVPS, which are rare, sometimes require surgery but for the majority of patients, symptoms are controlled through diet, exercise and natural supplements.

The diet aspect would be, to avoid stimulants in your diet (caffeine, alcohol, tobacco, stress and chocolate) that can be triggers for MVPS symptoms. Also a healthy diet with lots of fruits and vegetables is always a good idea. Also a good multi-vitamin helps the body's systems operate at a more optimal level. MVP patients may also need to take a "magnesium" supplement (mineral that helps with heart function) but need to have their magnesium level checked (mineral analysis) to see how much they need to be taking and only take the recommended amount as monitored by their doctor.

Exercise is also greatly helpful in regulating the "Involuntary Nervous System" (involved in heart function), as well as the heart rate, blood-pressure and anxiety symptoms. It can also help reduce stress that can contribute to symptoms. Exercise can be of more benefit than any other single factor but a patient must pace their self and only exercise at their tolerance-level, then increase that level as they are able.

Walking is a great way to begin an exercise program and even if you only increase the distance and/or briskness of your walk over time, the benefits can be tremendous.

Hyperthyroidism-Overactive Thyroid Gland

When a person's thyroid gland begins producing too much hormone, this causes the metabolism of the body to increase to an abnormally high level. When this happens, all functions in the body are sped-up including nervous system activity that regulates how much adrenaline is released by the adrenal glands. Because of the hyper metabolism, the blood pressure and heart rate increase to abnormal levels, causing the person to feel nervous, agitated and anxious.

Treatment for an overactive thyroid gland may include anti-thyroid medications that slow production of thyroid hormones, beta-blocker drugs that help with the effects of too much adrenaline and drugs that help control anxiety symptoms (anti-anxiety). If hyperthyroidism becomes severe and difficult to control, some patients may need their thyroid glands removed by surgery (thyroidectomy) or through destroying the gland by use of radioactive iodine (RAI Ablation).

Hyper-functioning Adrenal Glands-Hyperadrenalism

In some cases of overproduction of adrenal hormones, including adrenaline, there is a problem in the adrenal glands themselves. A normal person has two adrenal glands and in some cases there can be a tumor in one or both of the glands (adenoma) and this will cause stimulation of the gland in producing too much hormone. This would be a "primary" cause of adrenal hyper-function.

The Everything Anxiety-Coping Book!

Sometimes a chronic disease in the body or a tumor in another major endocrine gland (pituitary or hypothalamus) can cause adrenal hormone imbalance as described and in this case the hyper-functioning of the glands would be a "secondary" cause.

When overproduction of adrenal hormones is severe, the condition might be referred to as "Cushing's Disease." The treatment for overactive adrenal glands would include drugs that help reduce/control adrenal hormone production, removal of tumors or removal of one or both of the glands if necessary. If the adrenal glands are being overly stimulated by the master brain gland called the "pituitary," radiation therapy directed at that master brain gland may be used to slow its production of the "ACTH" hormone (Adrenocorticotropic Hormone). This hormone is sent from the pituitary to stimulate release of adrenal hormones and its activity may need to be slowed down if it is overactive in regulating/stimulating the adrenals.

Hypoglycemia

When blood glucose (sugar) levels fall too low, the condition is referred to as hypoglycemia. Glucose is normally converted into energy for the cells of the body via the hormone insulin, which carries it into these cells for use by the body. People whose bodies become resistant to insulin over time or those who do not eat regular meals may find that their glucose level has wide swings that may include these drops that result in symptoms, including those of anxiety and nervousness.

The reason a person may become anxious with hypoglycemic episodes is due to the body sending out more adrenaline in attempt to prompt the body the convert more energy. It is the body's way of trying to kick-start the energy conversion from glucose when it senses the level becomes too low.

When you read the lists of symptoms for hypoglycemia on medical sources, you'll find anxiety listed commonly and the treatment listed for it includes drugs that help regulate glucose (especially for diabetics), eating small regular meals, eliminating all foods that contain refined sugars (those not occurring naturally), limiting intake of foods high in natural sugars, weight loss/control and exercise. When anxiety symptoms are frequent or severe in people with hypoglycemia, they may also be prescribed anti-anxiety or antidepressant medications.

Hashitoxicosis

A major subject for me to write about is thyroid disease, especially the autoimmune type in which the immune system sends antibodies out to attack the thyroid gland. If you have thyroid disease, you may have experienced some co-morbid (related) anxiety along with it.

This can especially be true if you have autoimmune thyroid disease, which includes Graves' Disease/hyperthyroidism and Hashimoto'sthyroiditis/hypothyroidism, which can cause "Hashitoxicosis" (intermittent hyperthyroidism) early into its onset. Most cases of thyroid related anxiety symptoms are significantly resolved once thyroid hormone imbalances are corrected either through slowing down thyroid hormone production via "anti-thyroid drugs" or replacing low hormone levels via thyroid hormone replacement therapy.

Thyroid patients often report experiencing a "free floating" type anxiety, meaning a persistent level that causes them to feel on-edge and easily startled. A very unpleasant type of anxiety reaction they may also experience are "panic attacks" and if they are experienced frequently, it is referred to as "Panic Disorder". These are very unpleasant attacks that cause anxiety symptoms to escalate suddenly.

When people experience them, they will often hyperventilate and experience a racing heart and an extreme fear emotion. If you are experiencing panic attacks you are far from being alone. Estimates for the U.S. alone have identified approximately 6-million panic disorder sufferers and millions more suffer panic attacks at a slightly less frequency.

When correcting imbalanced thyroid hormones, does not significantly reduce anxiety symptoms, thyroid patients may be prescribed anti-anxiety and/or antidepressant drugs or may be referred for psychiatric therapy. Drug and therapies are also sometimes combined when patients are in need of both and some are later able to slowly discontinue the prescribed drugs as they learn better coping through psychiatric counseling.

Chapter 2.

More about Panic Disorder and Thyroid Disease

"Panic Attacks" are what you might describe as the "climax of anxiety" and are truly unpleasant, to say the least, as we who have experienced them know! They can occur with just about any other anxiety disorder, including Generalized Anxiety Disorder (GAD) but when the panic attacks themselves are the feature-manifestation as previously mentioned, it is referred to as "Panic Disorder" (PD). They can hit extremely hard and a person first experiencing them will commonly believe they are having a heart attack! Many people new to the experience find their selves in hospital emergency rooms, only to be told everything physically checks out normal, once they return to a calmed state.

The Everything Anxiety-Coping Book!

Many new to the panic experience will also believe they are going mad/insane or that another attack will cause them to completely lose control. It has been my experience and that of many other people I have corresponded with, to discover that the onset of severe anxiety symptoms would be revealed as thyroid disease. Most patients with thyroid disease (80%) end up with a low functioning thyroid or "hypothyroidism" but if it is the autoimmune type, the initial phase they may experience, is "hyperthyroidism" or an overactive thyroid (also true of temporary forms of thyroiditis). This hyperthyroid phase of Hashitoxicosis (short term thyrotoxicity) causes hyperthyroidism symptoms, such as anxiety, nervousness, sweating, weight loss etc... Afterward patients will revert back to hypothyroidism as a progressive condition.

Anxiety symptoms are one possible manifestation of hyperthyroidism or an over-active thyroid gland.

When a patient visits their Doctor with the symptoms described above combined with excessive energy, weight loss, hair loss, sweating, diarrhea and swelling or pain in their thyroid, blood tests of thyroid function should be ordered. This is true even if only one or two of these symptoms are present.

Thyroid disorders are one of the more common causes of both anxiety and depression symptoms. The thyroid gland regulates the metabolism of our bodies and affects every cell and organ. When a person's thyroid gland becomes either over-active (hyperthyroidism) or under-active (hypothyroidism), the results can be both physical and emotional symptoms.

The most common method used to diagnose thyroid disorders, is through blood testing. Blood is drawn and lab-tested to see if the thyroid's hormone levels are in the normal range. If they are outside of the normal reference range, on the high end, this would indicate an over-active thyroid gland, "hyperthyroidism".

If the hormone levels are found to be outside of the range on the low end, it would indicate an under-active thyroid gland, "hypothyroidism". It bears repeating that anxiety symptoms occur in both hypothyroid and hyperthyroid conditions.

There is another very sensitive thyroid function test available and one that many Doctors will use alone before testing the actual thyroid hormones and it is a test called "TSH" (Thyroid Stimulating Hormone). This particular one is not actually a thyroid hormone but one that comes from the "pituitary gland", a master endocrine gland found in the brain. This gland regulates the thyroid, which is found in the neck, just below the Adam's apple. The pituitary does this by means of the TSH hormone, which it sends to the thyroid to stimulate it to produce its own hormones, at the proper levels.

If TSH is found to be low, this would indicate that the thyroid gland is no longer being stimulated by the pituitary to produce hormones because it is already over-active.

The Everything Anxiety-Coping Book!

If TSH is found to be high, this would indicate that the pituitary is working too hard to get the thyroid to produce hormones because it is under-active. So TSH is a valuable test because of its sensitiveness in monitoring thyroid function.

If you suspect you have thyroid disease, that is either causing or aggravating anxiety symptoms in you, plus you experience some of the other symptoms that indicate possible thyroid dysfunction, talk to your Doctor about getting tested because if this is the cause, treatment will go a long way toward relieving anxiety symptoms.

Chapter 3.

Anxiety with Thyroid Hormone Therapy

If you experience some anxiety symptoms when starting thyroid hormone replacement for hypothyroidism, your case is not unusual, in fact this was my experience when being started on thyroid hormone therapy early in the year 2003 for an under active thyroid caused by Hashimoto's thyroiditis. Patients sometimes experience hyperthyroid type symptoms as their body adjusts to thyroid medication and can this feel worse when anxiety is already present to begin with. Some Doctors help patients through this adjustment period, by giving them an as-needed anti-anxiety medication, for use short-term. I say short-term because some of these as needed anti-anxiety medications can lead to dependency, if taken for more than a few weeks (i.e. benzodiazepines).

The Everything Anxiety-Coping Book!

Strangely, as mentioned, hypothyroidism can cause anxiety symptoms and some patients seem to experience anxiety when it is at the level between normal and sub-clinical (mildly low functioning). The hormone therapy actually takes a patient to that point between euthroid (normal hormone levels) and sub-clinical hypothyroidism before it goes on to correct the hypothyroidism. This is due to the fact that as the thyroid medication is brought into your system, from the outside (orally), your own thyroid begins to shut down any of its own production of thyroid hormone. Some refer to this as "suppression of the thyroid gland" or causing it to "atrophy" (dwindle down). Once a patient passes that break-even point on thyroid hormone therapy, they will then begin to see improvement in symptoms as the hypothyroidism is corrected from that point forward. It is an interesting phenomenon and is why it is referred to as thyroid hormone "replacement".

This is simply a theory on my part as a well-studied layperson on thyroid disease subjects but I believe that the in-between point of sub-clinical hypothyroidism and that of becoming euthroid, causes adrenal surges, much like people experience with hypoglycemia (low blood sugar). The body has an incredible system of sensors, which are neurotransmitters and hormones that communicate with each other and it knows how to compensate for hormonal changes.

My belief is that when the body senses small downward fluctuations in thyroid hormone, especially when a person it teetering between being euthroid and sub-clinically hypothyroid, the body tries to compensate for the hormone fluctuation, by releasing more adrenaline, as an alternative source of energy and to keep the body better kick-started. I also believe this is why hypothyroid patients at this point of sub-clinical hypothyroidism, will feel these adrenaline surges upon waking in the mornings and at other points during the day.

The Everything Anxiety-Coping Book!

This theory comes from my corresponding with literally 100s of thyroid patients, in addition to my own experience with this. It also comes from the reading of a number of medical research articles that clearly state that anxiety and anxiety disorders, can be related to hypothyroidism, especially the autoimmune type (Hashimoto's thyroiditis), the most common. Some published research also clearly associates anxiety with sub-clinical hypothyroidism.

You may need help in getting through that in-between stage with thyroid hormone therapy, if needed by taking a prescription as-needed anti-anxiety medication, to help you get through the process of reaching a euthroid state. Also, by self-educating yourself, you will lend towards better treatment for yourself as well by becoming a partner with your Doctor in working toward getting your hypothyroid treatment optimized for you as an individual and unique patient.

Chapter 4.

Medical Causes of Depression

Clinical depression often manifests co-morbid to anxiety disorders and conditions. People suffering depressive mood problems can experience the following symptoms.

• feeling profoundly sad

• hopeless

• empty

• a sense of desperation

• thoughts of suicide

• inability to enjoy activities that were once pleasurable

While many cases of depression are not related to medical conditions, there are cases in which health conditions and diseases can be a contributing cause.

The Everything Anxiety-Coping Book!

The subheadings below help us to understand four medical conditions that are often associated with causing depression.

Hypothyroidism

With an under-active thyroid gland, the body's metabolism is slowed down causing mental activity to slow down as well. This contributes to symptoms of depression in people who have hypothyroidism or who are in the process of developing it. The brain as well as all other organs in the body are affected by lack of thyroid hormone production and this causes the level of an important neurotransmitter called "serotonin" to also become low. Depression symptoms usually improve significantly when the low hormone is replaced through prescribed drug therapy.

For those hypothyroid patients who have stubborn depression symptoms that remain unrelieved after thyroid hormone replacement, their doctors may prescribe SSRI drugs (Selective Serotonin Reuptake Inhibitors) that increase serotonin levels or other antidepressant medications. Doctors may also refer their patients to mental health professionals for therapy that can also help. Hypothyroidism is one of several metabolic conditions that can result in symptoms of depression.

Pain Syndromes

There are a number of health conditions and diseases that cause widespread body pain in people who have them. This includes syndromes such as Fibromyalgia and Chronic Fatigue Syndrome, both of which have joint and muscle aches as part of their symptom-manifestations.

Other conditions that cause chronic pain include various types of arthritis, including Osteoarthritis (the most common type) and Rheumatoid Arthritis which is, the autoimmune type causing varied degrees of joint destruction.

All of these conditions have the potential to cause depression symptoms due to their ability to increase the stress levels of those who suffer with them because of ongoing pain. Treatment for these conditions may include use of pain medications and anti-inflammatory drugs, which when administered, can also result in improved emotions in patients whose pain levels are reduced by them. Addition of SSRI antidepressants or psychological therapies may also be suggested for patients who may also need them.

Anemia

When the blood of an individual has become weakened due to loss of an adequate number of red blood cells or due to a reduction in the size of them, the condition is called "anemia". There are a number of different types of anemia, including that commonly caused by iron deficiency and those caused by deficiencies of substances such as ferritin, folic acid or vitamin B12 levels. When anemia occurs, the blood becomes less oxygenated and this causes the person experiencing it to have severe fatigue and inadequate functioning of all body organs, including the brain.

Medical sources commonly list depression as a symptom of anemia, as well as fatigue, muscle weakness and loss of appetite. The treatments for anemia include replacing the element, vitamin or nutrient that has become low and that is resulting in the anemic condition.

Patients with anemia may also benefit from drugs or therapies that help with depression symptoms, should medical treatments fail to fully accomplish this.

Anxiety Disorders

While people suffering chronic anxiety, may be experiencing an emotional-only disorder not related to a medical condition, others may have health disorders that contribute to or actually cause their anxiety disorder as previously discussed. Regardless of the cause of severe anxiety states, they also have the potential to cause associated depression symptoms. Mental health authorities often state that anxiety disorders commonly cause co-occurring depression. With this being the case, depression often lifts in these individuals when their anxiety condition is treated. The treatments commonly administered to anxiety patients include anti-anxiety medications, SSRI and other types of antidepressants and psychological therapies including Cognitive Behavioral Therapy (CBT).

The Everything Anxiety-Coping Book!

If you are experiencing the symptoms of depression, see your doctor as soon as possible to receive a diagnosis of the cause and information on treatments that are available.

<u>Chapter 5.</u>

Is "Nervous Breakdown" a True Medical Term?

This subject was covered within a previous section however, this chapter, originally written as a separate article, includes additional perspectives.

A nervous breakdown in reality means you have been limited in carrying on daily activities due to the onset of severe stress or an emotional disorder. Medical doctors and mental health professionals seldom use the term nervous breakdown but will give a more specific diagnosis.

The term "nervous breakdown" is actually not widely recognized by mental health professionals or by those in the medical profession.

The term became popular in modern culture as a type of catch-all phrase describing a condition experienced by people who were suffering from the aftereffects of traumatic events or who were emotionally distraught or experiencing an overwhelming level of stress. Many times these people were coined as having a nervous breakdown in order to avoid disclosing the personal details of their lives. Hollywood actors and actresses who were overworked and became overwhelmed by their schedules, requiring them to take time off were often described as having nervous breakdowns.

People who experience anxiety disorders and clinical depression were at one time described as having nervous breakdowns. As mental health and medical professionals have gained more knowledge of anxiety disorders and clinical depression over the years, they have been able to give a diagnosis of these disorders specifically to people who were once thought to be suffering a nervous breakdown.

The aspect of limitation to some people with emotional disorders that leaves them unable to continue normally with daily activities is what brought the belief to others around them that they were suffering or had suffered a nervous breakdown.

In reality, nerves and the nervous system cannot break down or burn out unless they are being destroyed by a neurological disease process. Stress, anxiety and depression are not in the neurological disease category but are chronic and severe disorders involving the mind and emotions. Emotional disorders that were at one time commonly thought of as nervous breakdowns include Post Traumatic Stress Disorder, Agoraphobia, Generalized Anxiety Disorder, Panic Disorder and Major/Clinical Depression.

There are methods for helping to avoid emotional disorders that might be perceived as nervous breakdowns.

Avoiding chronic emotional problems means you are preventing the onset of severe anxiety and depression from setting in and bringing limitations to your life. Stress is directly linked to both anxiety and depression and methods for reducing and avoiding stress are important and include those listed below (more on this in the final chapter).

• relaxation and meditation techniques

• stretching type exercises (i.e. Yoga, Tai Chi and Deep Breathing)

• simple mild exercise of any type

• taking short relaxation breaks at home and at work

• getting enough sleep and rest

Practicing these methods helps one to avoid emotional problems that might be perceived as a nervous breakdown to those around them.

If you experience an emotional disorder, there are treatments to help you to recover or to cope significantly. If stress overwhelms you or if you experience a traumatic event in your life that results in severe emotional problems, it is very important to see your doctor about treatment options. Emotional disorders are serious in that they can continue to restrict one's life, as was evident when they were referred to as nervous breakdowns in the past. Doctors can prescribe medications to help control anxiety and/or depression symptoms but they may also refer patients to mental health practitioners for recommended therapies.

Most mental health professionals are called psychiatrists or psychologists and they have many different therapy methods to help people with emotional disorders cope and to regain the normal activities of life. Some people may be treated with combinations of both medication and emotional therapy.

The Everything Anxiety-Coping Book!

One highly successful method of therapy is called Cognitive Behavioral Therapy (CBT) which has had a very high success rate for people with both anxiety and depressive disorders.

If you feel you are heading toward an emotional disorder (nervous breakdown) or believe you have already experienced the onset of one, do not delay in inquiring with your doctor regarding treatment options.

Chapter 6.

Coping Methods for Anxiety Disorders and Major Depression

The following chapter was originally written as suggested coping methods for Generalized Anxiety Disorder (GAD) however, the methods are also effective for helping treat depression. GAD, is in-fact the anxiety disorder that commonly has co-occurring (co-existing) depression that can be experienced with it. The methods following below include aspects of Cognitive Behavioral Therapy, Relaxation Techniques and Thought Diversion Methods.

Generalized Anxiety Disorder is a common anxiety condition affecting approximately 6.8 million Americans. The type of anxiety found in this condition is a severe and ongoing (chronic) type of worry, lasting at least six months. People with GAD also tend to worry irrationally over things that the average person would see as insignificant.

The Everything Anxiety-Coping Book!

It also commonly has aspects of Major
Depressive Disorder that co-exists with it. There
are methods for helping cope with this
sometimes disabling anxiety disorder as
addressed in the subheadings below.

**Remind yourself that worrying about problems
or potential ones will not help to diminish them.**

People with GAD tend to believe that by not
pondering their problems, they are not staying
prepared to deal with them and so they will
ruminate constantly about their existing
problems and about those that might arise. This
causes them to become stressed out and unable
to function at their best level when working,
studying and attending to family duties. A type of
self therapy that is often used in methods such as
Cognitive Behavioral Therapy (CBT) is to reassure
one's self that this type worry is irrational and far
exceeds that which these problems are deserving
of.

By either repeating this in the mind or by actually speaking reassuring-type thoughts aloud to yourself, you can help calm the worried thoughts and bring them more under control.

It might also be helpful to actually write these reassuring thoughts on paper and carry them with you for reading to yourself at times worried thoughts begin to crop up. Reassuring thoughts that can be helpful would be for example to say, "I'm in control of any problems that might arise; they are not in control of me" or "I refuse to sweat the small stuff because it is all small stuff" or "My worry will not diminish my problems and they will all wait until I'm ready to deal with them at another time". There are CBT programs available online or you may ask your doctor to refer you to one that can help you learn these methods.

Use distractions to take your mind off of worried or depressing thoughts.

An effective method for accomplishing this step would be to replace thoughts of worry with ones about your accomplishments, your blessings in life such as family, friends and things you can look forward to such as retirement, your children and your grandchildren. Replace worried thoughts with anything that brings you peace of mind, positive excitement and pleasurable experiences. This is of course easier said than done at those times you're tempted to worry but it can be accomplished with practice.

Taking time to reflect on good memories of things you have experienced in life can also be an effective distraction to help your mind not gravitate toward worry-thoughts. Reflecting back on good memories from your childhood, the courtship of your spouse and other good times you've had with family and friends can help train your mind to think positively and to avoid negative thought processes/patterns.

The Everything Anxiety-Coping Book!

Give yourself leisure time to enjoy things that help relax your mind.

This requires giving yourself permission to enjoy hobbies, sports and other types of leisure activities that help keep your mind in a more relaxed state. Remember that everyone needs time to unwind and relax and that the human body and mind require rest, relaxation and enjoyment, which helps to keep us balanced rather than stressed out, nervous, anxious and in a state of chronic worry. Remind yourself that you deserve these types of restful activities because you spend enough time working and attending to the other duties and struggles of life.

Things that people find help them to have relaxed minds include being involved in the arts, such as painting, sculpting and writing.

Others find relaxation being involved in the following types of activities.

• outdoors activities (i.e. fishing, hiking and camping)

• mild exercise

• horseback riding

• watching enjoyable movies

Whatever you may choose to pursue as leisure activity, your goal will be to find those things that help your mind to relax rather than having it ponder on duties or problems that should be addressed at more appropriate times.

If GAD or depression symptoms become overwhelming, ask your doctor about medications that can help.

Taking a prescribed drug for emotional symptoms that you find difficult to cope with on your own is nothing to be ashamed of as mentioned in previous chapters. Drugs such as permanent or as-needed anti-anxiety medications and SSRI antidepressants may become necessary if chronic worry or depression caused by GAD is too severe to cope with on your own. Admitting you need the extra help is admirable and you should not be embarrassed if you are in need of a medication to help with your anxiety. Millions of people need medications of these types to help them better cope with anxiety disorders and depression and you are far from being alone.

Also remember that these type medications are not always needed permanently and there may come a time that you are able to cope using therapy methods and will be able to discontinue the medication. Should such a time come, you and your doctor will recognize this and can work on a schedule for a gradual discontinued use of the drug(s).

Pace yourself so that your schedule doesn't become overwhelming to you.

People with GAD have a tendency to push themselves too hard by taking on too many tasks at a time. Their perceived need to do this comes from their worry that they will get behind on their duties, causing them to mount and to become too difficult to manage. This is a scenario that should be avoided by GAD sufferers because constant multitasking will result in becoming stressed out due to feeling overwhelmed with the many duties being performed.

The Everything Anxiety-Coping Book!

Ways to avoid taking on too many duties would be to avoid any unnecessary commitments and to write down a manageable schedule and to abide by it as closely as possible. When performing a job for an employer, a GAD sufferer should remind himself that a reasonable amount of performance is what his job requires and he should not have to overextend himself. Most employers want their employees to pace their work because the quality of it is usually more important than the quantity.

If you find yourself struggling with abnormally severe worry or find yourself worrying about things in an irrational manner, see your doctor for an evaluation. If your doctor diagnoses you with GAD and possibly co-occurring depression, the methods listed above may be a helpful part of a treatment regimen.

If you suffer chronic anxiety or depression symptoms that you suspect may be related to a medical condition, see your doctor for further evaluation. Even if you feel the anxiety and/or depression is not associated with another condition, your doctor can suggest options that will help treat your symptoms.

Section Four: **Identifying and Treating Mental and Emotional Disorders**

<u>Chapter 1.</u>

The Differences between Psychosis and Common Anxiety and Depression

Common anxiety and clinical depression are types of "neurosis".

Psychosis is the term for a mental disorder that causes a person to lose touch with reality and that may cause them to have hallucinations and delusions. Mental disorders that are in the psychosis category include bipolar disorder and schizophrenia.

Anxiety and common clinical depression are both in the neurosis category, meaning they are stress and nerve-related and not caused by a severe underlying mental disorder.

Persons with severe forms of depression, such as bipolar disorder, may have psychotic episodes but your more common type of clinical depression and anxiety disorders are not in the psychosis category, but rather are types of neurosis (psychoneurosis). According to the National Institute of Mental Health, psychosis affects an estimated 1% of the U.S. population, while the more common anxiety and depression conditions affect a much higher percentage. Perhaps as many as 1 in 4 or 25% of the American population experience an anxiety disorder and/or clinical depression at some time during their lives.

Anxiety-related "depersonalization" and "de-realization" can be mistaken for psychotic episodes.

Depersonalization is an anxiety-induced experience where a person feels he or she is "unreal" or no longer exists as a person. They may even feel they are no longer visible to other people and that others around them remain real but they no longer are. Some patients describe it as feeling like they are watching their own actions from outside of themselves, and they no longer feel like a human being but have become robotic. Patients have described episodes, for example, of looking at their own face in a mirror and wondering if they are really there. They may also feel as if they no longer recognize themselves and feel as if they are having an identity crisis.

De-realization, is similar, except that the person's surroundings seem to lose reality.

With de-realization, an anxiety sufferer will have episodes of experiencing feelings that their surroundings have become unreal. They may also feel as if reality itself is no longer something they can fully recognize during these moments. They may also question the reality of many things at these times, and may begin to wonder if life is simply a dream of some type. Some anxiety sufferers describe this experience as being like "living inside a bubble", or like they are trying to see everything through a haze or a thick fog. This is also referred to as "brain fog" when it hinders the ability for a person to concentrate with the same sharpness, as when they are nor experiencing unreality symptoms.

Anxiety sufferers need to understand the fact that these de-realization and depersonalization symptoms do not indicate that they are going insane or actually losing touch with reality. They are sensations rather than an actual manifestation of losing touch with reality in the true sense, as occurs with psychotic illnesses.

They are both very common occurrences in anxiety sufferers, especially in those who experience panic attacks and will not cause damage to a person's mind or sanity. This fear of going insane is a very concerning one to people who experience severe anxiety and panic, and also to those who experience major/clinical depression. Indeed, anxiety and panic often co-exist, but these are irrational thoughts that will not happen.

The major features of bipolar disorder are different from common clinical depression.

The name "bipolar disorder" describes "two opposite extremes". People with this mental disorder will have episodes of severe depressed mood, followed by episodes of manic behavior (*mania*, meaning periods of extreme, elated feelings). In fact during manic episodes, a bipolar person may seem full of energy and want to go on late-night shopping sprees for example, or work on a new project for long hours.

The Everything Anxiety-Coping Book!

They may also go without sleep for many days or even weeks at a time. Bipolar depressive disorder was previously referred to as "manic depression" because of the episodes of mania that are a characteristic feature of it.

Bipolar disorder patients tend to feel self-exalted at these manic times, thinking they are very special and greater/stronger than the average person, which is a type of delusional thinking. Some bipolar people have "mixed episodes", in which these severely depressed and manic spells may cycle more rapidly.

Anxiety sufferers may experience episodes of "catastrophic thinking", but this symptom is also not related to true psychosis.

Catastrophic thinking also happens to many anxiety sufferers and is also referred to as the "what ifs" (fear of possible events).

The Everything Anxiety-Coping Book!

Anxiety disorder patients describe thoughts of losing control of their selves in front of others and making their selves look silly or foolish. Other patients may experience a fear that they might pass out and need the aid of an ambulance, but not be found in time by someone who can call one for them. Other anxiety sufferers have described fears of snapping and committing violence to other people around them, or that they might run down a grocery store isle, screaming or fall to the floor and curl up in a ball.

One of the reasons catastrophic thinking is also unpleasant is because these fearful thoughts can increase and intensify the already-present anxiety symptoms. Catastrophic thinking, in fact, can be a trigger for panic episodes in some people who struggle with it. This "what if" thinking tends to lead from one thought to another, until many fearful thoughts are all happening simultaneously, which could be referred to as a snowball type of effect.

The thoughts gain momentum and grow larger and scarier to the anxiety sufferer, as they increase during episodes of intense anxiety.

Common anxiety and depression can have serious symptoms of their own, but they do not cause patients to become delusional or hallucinate in the true sense. This is the major difference between neurosis and psychosis.

Recognizing Bipolar Disorder

Recently, while moderating on a thyroid disease, patient-forum, someone posted about being diagnosed by an MD, with "Bipolar Disorder" and they were prescribed an anti-psychotic drug for this. While these type drugs are extremely needful and very helpful to people who do truly need them for disorders of psychosis they may be suffering, at the same time, I believe any patient in doubt about a diagnosis of this type, should seek confirmation of needing such a drug.

Sometimes a second opinion by a qualified mental health professional is needed because these drugs are powerful and designed for a specific purpose and should only be prescribed to patients who actually have psychotic disorders or episodes.

Below is my response to this individual, in regard to Bipolar Disorder and in regard their being prescribed drugs for this, despite their concerns that the diagnosis could possibly be incorrect. Some of my response to this, came from my own experience in seeing family members diagnosed with psychotic disorders they did not have and from an experience years ago, when this was also my personal experience. Following below, is the reply I gave this person who posted on that forum:

Response:

"While I certainly believe these type drugs can be of tremendous value to people who have Bi-Polar Disorder or schizophrenia, I also know that for reasons we may never know, there are Doctors who are prescribing some of these anti-psychotic drugs to people who do not have the disorders the drugs are designed to treat. I believe the prescription drug "Depakote" that your Doctor is prescribing for you, is also used to treat epilepsy and migraine headaches.

I know a little about the phenomenon of non-confirmed diagnosis of mental disorders because I have a nephew and aunt on opposite sides of my family, who were both "diagnosed" with bi-polar and schizophrenia and neither of them had either of these disorders. Their incorrect diagnoses were corrected once they were evaluated further by qualified mental health professionals.

The Everything Anxiety-Coping Book!

In regard to my personal experience in this area, in the late 1980s, I had a very bad job situation and developed anxiety and a stomach malady due to the stress of it and upon seeing an MD; he diagnosed me with manic depression (an early term for bi-polar disorder). He prescribed me an anti-psychotic drug, which I only took for one month, until my Church Pastor, made me realize it was a bogus diagnosis and he proved this by showing me a medical resource describing the condition in-detail. I experienced severe side effects from the drug as well, during my short term use of it. My symptoms did not even remotely point to bi-polar but were typical anxiety symptoms, which resolved after a job change, to a less stressful occupation.

Let me just say that with bi-polar, the name describes just what it is, "two opposed extremes". People with it, will become severely depressed, and followed by episodes of "mania" as previously described.

The point being, that if you do not experience spells of mania/extreme elation, it is unlikely Bi-polar Disorder. Another reason I know this is because I have witnessed the episodes experienced by people who are bi-polar and it is fairly obvious when a person actually has this mental disorder.

Depression alternating with anxiety is not the same thing. These two commonly co-exist but anxiety is not mania, it is a fear emotion, that also causes chronic worry at times and certainly this would not be an elated or exalting feeling.

In regard to schizophrenia, this mental disorder is characterized by episodes of hallucinations, delusional thinking and losing touch with reality. Patients with this condition can many times have their psychosis well controlled through anti-psychotic medications and they can live relatively normal lives. This does vary however among patients, according to the severity of their disorders.

The Everything Anxiety-Coping Book!

In more severe cases patients may be required to receive ongoing professional care in a mental health facility.

Neither bipolar nor schizophrenic patients are "crazy" or "insane". These are unfair and inconsiderate characterizations of them. These patients are experiencing mental illnesses, of no fault of their own and can be as high quality in their character and as intelligent as anyone who does not suffer mental illness.

I would be very cautious when doubting a suspect-diagnosis to add such a drug (anti-psychotic prescription) to your treatment regimen and for a more definitive, substantiated diagnosis I would see a mental health professional before accepting one offered by an MD or GP who does not specialize in mental health.

Anxiety and depression affect a very large percent of the population, while bi-polar and schizophrenia affect approximately 1%.

ALSO: yes, depression and anxiety both are strongly connected and are common symptoms of thyroid disease as you asked in your question. Bi-polar is believed to have a connection to thyroid disease as well but as I describe above, it must meet the mania criteria to be diagnosed bi-polar disorder. Depakote, in my understanding is designed to control the mania aspect of the disorder.

Regular MDs and GPs, in my opinion, should be cautious in diagnosing common anxiety and depression, as psychotic disorders."
(End of Reply)

Chapter 2.

Cognitive Behavioral Therapy for Anxiety Disorders

Anxiety Disorders include Panic Disorder, Obsessive-Compulsive Disorder, Post-Traumatic Stress Disorder, Generalized Anxiety Disorder, and Phobias (social phobia, agoraphobia, and specific phobia).

Approximately 40 million American adults ages 18 and older, or about 18.1 percent of people in this age group in a given year, have an anxiety disorder.

Anxiety disorders frequently co-occur with depressive disorders or substance abuse.

Most people with one anxiety disorder also have another anxiety disorder. Nearly three-quarters of those with an anxiety disorder will have their first episode by age 21. (Statistics are from the U.S. NIMH)

The Everything Anxiety-Coping Book!

One of the more successful treatments for anxiety symptoms and anxiety disorders is a method of therapy called "Cognitive Behavioral Therapy" (CBT) and many anxiety disorder patients have had great success in <u>overcoming</u> and <u>coping</u> with anxiety symptoms through this method.

Some aspects of CBT that are important parts of the therapy include:

Change the way the patient thinks about anxiety in general and about the symptoms it causes.

The patient will learn through this aspect of CBT that anxiety itself is a "natural emotion". The unpleasantness of the symptoms in people in whom anxiety has become a "disorder" comes from the fact that this normal emotion can occur out of context or at inappropriate times (disordered).

When a patient learns that the emotion he is experiencing is not "strange or foreign," this alone can help toward reducing the fear of the symptoms anxiety disorder causes. Once a patient with anxiety accepts the fact the emotion is natural and is supposed to occur at the appropriate times, he can:

Look at those things that have become "triggers" in causing anxiety to occur out of context or in a disordered fashion.

One way to express this fact to an anxiety sufferer is to say; "Anxiety is a completely natural and normal emotion and it is only the <u>timing</u> of it that has become out of the order it was intended to happen." Under normal circumstances, the anxiety emotion was created to be triggered in order to allow the one experiencing it to have the sudden added strength and presence of mind, to flee from danger or to fight an enemy that has attacked him. This is the origin of the term for triggered-anxiety that is referred to as the "fight or flight" response).

The Everything Anxiety-Coping Book!

Recognize that anxiety also gives added abilities, determination and ambition to the one who experiences it, in order for him to perform a task at hand.

This can be any task that requires what some might also call "intestinal fortitude" - that internal strength we all have and must call upon at times, as it is needed. Everyone has important tasks to perform in their everyday lives and at times we also experience emergency situations or those with important priorities involved. Firemen must be on alert to put out fires that are called in to them, teachers must have the inspiration to interest their pupils in learning the subjects being studied, and an athlete in a track meet must be ready to run in an attempt to win a race. Without the anxiety emotion, they would not have the added strength and inspiration to accomplish these tasks as successfully.

The Everything Anxiety-Coping Book!

A person who is called upon to make a public speech for example, needs that extra inspiration to bring forth his spoken points more powerfully and with conviction. Anxiety is what adds to this experience and helps them to accomplish this. The butterflies in the stomach and sweaty hands can actually be a sign that you one is about to make a powerful presentation and not that they are about to run off of the stage due to stage-fright and so, it is all in how one looks at it. You can make anxiety responses work for you or work against you. Will you see it as positive energy to help inspire you or as fear that is holding you back? That is the question. Herein lies the secret to this aspect of Cognitive Behavioral Therapy; the way in which one perceives the anxiety they are experiencing!

Remember that there is no right or wrong in how one experiences anxiety; everyone is different.

When a group of people ride on a roller coaster at the amusement park, some will experience anxiety as an extreme fear-emotion while others on the same ride will experience it as welcome excitement. The types of people, who enjoy the adrenaline rush, also experience some fear with their excitement, but they actually enjoy it! They actually enjoy being scared occasionally and are the types of people who also like to take in a suspense thriller movie or horror film to get that same type of thrill. They are exhilarated by these experiences and one term used to describe them is "adrenaline junkies." If anxiety sufferers can learn to view anxiety in a different light and recognize it as a natural emotion, then they can better begin to use it to their advantage.

Getting anxiety to work more for you and less against you.

Is this more easily-said-than-done for people whose anxiety has developed into a disorder? Of course it is, but anything worthwhile takes time and effort to accomplish. An anxiety disorder sufferer who works on this important aspect will see small gains that will encourage him to continue in changing his perceptions about anxiety and over time, will begin to see a cumulative improvement in many areas of life that were previously affected negatively by anxiety.

An online search using "Cognitive Behavioral Therapy" as the search-term will yield lots of quality, reputable CBT programs that are available. Most are very affordable and well worth the cost for those seeking coping skills for anxiety disorders.

<u>Chapter 3.</u>

The Basic Differences between Anxiety & Depression

Anxiety and depression have a lot of similarities and some are even of the opinion that these are the same type fear-emotions that simply manifest differently in different people.

When you look at a list of symptoms for each there are indeed a great deal of similarities between them. Both can manifest with the following in-common symptoms.

• feelings of hopelessness

• agitation

• feeling withdrawn

• fatigue

• lack of ambition

The Everything Anxiety-Coping Book!

- inability to enjoy things that used to bring pleasure

- fear of the future

- inability to cope with stressful situations

It is also true that anxiety and depression often co-exist, in fact persons with actual anxiety disorders almost always have a degree of depression, along with it and persons with clinical depression commonly have a degree of co-existing anxiety.

So what would be considered some major distinguishing features of each? The fact is, that many times they are not easily distinguishable, in fact many Doctors, such as MDs that are not also psychiatrists or psychologists (mental health specialists), many times find it difficult to distinguish between them, so many times they will diagnose a patient with common emotional manifestations, as described above, as being a combination of both anxiety and depression or a "mixed emotional disorder".

The Everything Anxiety-Coping Book!

One Anxiety Disorder that is more-so a mix of both anxiety and depression, than the others that exist, is "Generalized Anxiety Disorder". With this type anxiety, patients commonly experience a mix of both anxiety and depression. They may at times have stronger manifestations of depression and at other times, stronger manifestations of anxiety, while yet at other times, they are both about even in manifestation.

So what would be a major distinguishing feature of each that helps us to recognize the difference between the two? A major distinguishing feature of depression that is often listed as one of its major symptoms is "profound sadness". An anxiety sufferer sometimes experiences spells of emotion, that causes them to have crying spells etc.., but it is not the same profound sadness that is more chronically severe with depression.

Anxiety sufferers on the other hand, have as a major feature of it, the "fear emotion", which can be the bewildering type, such as severe anxiety attacks or panic attacks or can be the chronic lingering type that manifests as chronic worry or severe apprehension.

The chronic worry aspect of anxiety, is what is most often mistakenly referred to as depression, when it is actually a fear emotion; fear of the future, fear about health, finances etc..., and though it is not in the depression category, it can result in depression, due to the prolonged periods of stress it causes.

To better illustrate this, let's look at a couple of example scenarios, following below.

In the first example scenario, we have a man, with a very important business meeting coming up. In this meeting, he will be required to convince the heads of his company, that his past accomplishments merit him a promotion to a more important position with the firm.

The Everything Anxiety-Coping Book!

The meeting is scheduled for two weeks away and yet the man has such hopes in doing well at the meeting, that he worries himself sick, during the entire two weeks leading up to the meeting. Family or friends observing his period of chronic worry, might make the observation, saying; "He sure has been depressed these past two weeks." The fact is that the man was experiencing a manifestation of anxiety, called chronic or obsessive worry, being triggered by a fear of failure.

In a second example scenario, we have a woman who does lose a long held position she had with a prestigious firm. This causes her to sink into a deep feeling of profound loss, that she feels she cannot recuperate from emotionally. She has continual feelings of sadness and has constant crying spells. An observer of her situation and resulting emotional state, remarks; "She has just been a bundle of nerves since losing her job and she's really going through an anxious time right now."

The Everything Anxiety-Coping Book!

In reality, the woman's experience is more-so in the depression category because she is experiencing profound sadness over losing her long held position with the firm.

While we may be able to better-place these examples of emotional scenarios into either the anxiety or depression categories, we also realize that both of these people very likely experienced aspects of both emotions to some degree. Again, this demonstrates how closely related these emotions are and how they often co-exist and how they can also fuel each other, causing worsening symptoms of each.

Fortunately, there are treatments that can help to diminish the symptoms of both emotional disorders simultaneously, such as SSRI Antidepressants, designed to help patients who experience both anxiety and depression, or either of them. There are also treatments, such as "Cognitive Behavioral Therapy", that offers coping and overcoming skills, for both anxiety and depression.

The Everything Anxiety-Coping Book!

Chapter 4.

Antidepressants Effective for some but not for Others

Before I begin the next subheadings and chapters in regard to SSRI antidepressants and other psychotropic drugs, I feel it is important that I make it very clear that I believe in the effectiveness of these type drugs for the right patients and within the proper cases/circumstances. I in-fact have close relatives who take these type prescribed drugs for anxiety disorders and major depression and they benefit significantly from them. Some patients in less common cases cannot adjust properly to certain types of these drugs however and must be given trials of different kinds to find the one that is appropriate for them.

The Everything Anxiety-Coping Book!

The following are types of psychotropic drugs (anti-anxiety and antidepressant) that are commonly prescribed to help patients with mood disorder symptoms.

- Paxil (paroxetine)

- Prozac (fluoxetine)

- Zoloft (sertraline)

- Wellbutrin (buproprion)

- Effexor (venlafaxine)

- Klonopin (clonazepam)

- Ativan (lorazepam)

- BuSpar (buspirone)

- Valium (diazepam)

- Xanax (alprazolam)

If the drug you're taking, is not working as it should, as prescribed for anxiety, depression or mixed emotional disorder or it is causing unwanted side effects, you may need to discuss with your Doctor, slowly weaning off of the drug and considering a trial of an "as-needed" anti-anxiety medication. These can be taken short-term, rather than the type that must be built-up in your system and maintained as a daily, permanent regimen. The fact is that some patients do fine with long-term antidepressants, while others do not.

Some Doctors seem to believe SSRI drugs (selective serotonin reuptake inhibitors) and other types of antidepressants work well for everyone but this simply is not true. I have corresponded with dozens of thyroid patients since the year 2003, who simply could not adjust well to them even after several months of trying to benefit from them, while many others report doing very well on them.

People are individuals and nothing works exactly the same for everyone and is a common sense approach that both Doctors and patients should take with these type drugs.

Blood Testing Before Prescribing Antidepressants

I was one of those patients who, was suspected of having emotional problems, not being caused by an underlying medical problem. I ended up requesting my own blood tests because I suspected a medical problem or disease, even expressing this, to the first Doctor I went to with my symptom complaints.

The combination of antidepressant, anti-anxiety medication and beta-blocker, that the first Doctor prescribed me in spite of my suggestion that I did not have an emotional-only disorder, did not help me.

My symptoms actually became worse until my underlying thyroid disease was diagnosed and treated. Doctors are human and capable of mistakes like everyone else but it is situations like these that point to the need for more education by the general public on the importance of diagnostic testing for underlying medical conditions.

Many times anxiety and/or depression does not have a medical cause but if a patient has other physical symptoms that indicate a possible co morbid disease, they should have blood testing ordered to determine if a medical condition is the cause, or to rule it out. Treating symptoms alone, without treating an underlying medical condition that is causing them, will only do so much good or possibly none all. In a worst case scenario, medications for anxiety and depression alone, while leaving an underlying disease untreated may actually cause the patient's condition to become worse.

The Everything Anxiety-Coping Book!

Medical blood testing is typically not that expensive, so should be ordered, so that if a medical condition does exist, it can be treated and the resulting effect will be improvement of all symptoms, including the emotional ones. If a patient needs the addition of medications to help with emotional symptoms, this can also be considered between the Doctor and patient, at the appropriate time during the treatment process.

One disease for example, that commonly causes anxiety and depression as part of its symptoms is thyroid disease as previously mentioned that affected me and that can result in hyperthyroidism (over-active thyroid) in some patients and hypothyroidism (under-active thyroid) in others. Of course there are many other diseases that cause emotional symptoms as well, as was covered in preceding chapters and subheadings.

Dr. Richard Hall MD and a professor of psychiatry, who has been involved in research studies at major medical universities such as John Hopkins University, has found in his studies, a direct relationship between anxiety and endocrine disorders. It was found in one study he directed, that in patients with "Hashimoto's thyroiditis/disease" (common autoimmune cause of hypothyroidism), anxiety was a common, initial and prominent symptom at the time patients were diagnosed.

There are also studies that have been published on the "PubMed" (U.S. National Institutes of Health) website, which is provided by the National Library of Medicine, that state that anxiety symptoms and anxiety disorders are directly associated with Hashimoto's disease. This is in addition to depression, which has been known to be a symptom of thyroid diseases for many years.

I believe if a hypothyroid patient for example, is on adequate treatment/hormone replacement therapy but still needs the added help of an antidepressant, there is nothing at all wrong with this! Having said this, let me now point out problems I see with Doctors who do not first give thyroid hormone replacement time to work, before adding an antidepressant to a patient's treatment. Certainly thyroid hormone therapy and any other hormone therapy, has the potential to relieve symptoms greatly. I'll say in my own case for example, that the emotional symptoms were the ones helped the most and the first to resolve when I was treated for thyroid disease and this alone was a great accomplishment for me.

Help with prescribed medication for anxiety, is nothing to be ashamed of or afraid of, if it is needed while your thyroid treatment is being optimized, which can actually take several months.

Dose adjustments are often needed, for as much as a year after beginning an initial dose. Some medical sources imply that thyroid hormone replacement therapy for hypothyroid conditions, takes only 4 to 6 weeks to do its job properly but this simply is not true with a large percent of patients, who may need several dosage adjustments for months, before they reach their optimal treatment level.

What was not good in my case and that has been found to be the case with other fellow thyroid patients I have corresponded with, who have basically experienced the same scenario as I, is the "snap diagnosed" for emotional-only problems that can occur. In my case thyroid disease was not blood-tested for until I demanded that the tests be ordered. Because of this, my fatigue, joint pain, dry skin, etc...., did not improve on the antidepressant alone but actually worsened. This combination of worsening hypothyroidism and the side effects of the SSRI-antidepressant I was prescribed resulted in my weaning off the drug very slowly.

In the mean time, blood tests I demanded and that blood was drawn for, just prior to starting the mood drugs, clearly revealed thyroid disease, including hypothyroidism and highly elevated thyroid antibody levels (thyroid autoimmunity).

The problem I saw in my original doctor pushing constantly for me to resume the antidepressant, along with my thyroid hormone medication, was that there was the potential for me to confuse the SSRI side-effects, with unrelieved thyroid disease symptoms. The side-effects after all, include some that are identical to thyroid disease, including: "fatigue, tremor, nervousness, lightheadedness etc..."

In my opinion, thyroid disease symptoms, including depression and/or anxiety, should be monitored in correlation with hormone treatment, to see how well they improve. If they do not begin to improve significantly after a few weeks on the administered, prescription therapy, an SSRI and other medications, such as those for muscle/joint aches etc..., can then be added.

I believe if anxiety and/or depression is thyroid disease related, obviously hormone replacement has an even greater potential to improve it, than an antidepressant does. This is not to say that a combination of these treatments might not be needed at some point.

Another problem is "withdrawal" from SSRI drugs and other medications designed to treat emotional disorders. Patients, who have been on an antidepressant for months or years, will experience a worsening of their emotional symptoms, plus other withdrawal symptoms, when weaning off of an antidepressant and this is why it must be done very slowly under doctor supervision. They may mistakenly believe this indicates that the emotional symptoms are becoming more severe without the SSRI or other drug, when in reality, this is a common reaction (worsening emotions and other withdrawal side-effects) when tapering off of one.

If a patient, with Doctor-supervision decides to taper off of an antidepressant, it must be done very slowly, with withdrawal symptoms monitored-for closely because some patients actually have been known to become suicidal during withdrawal, while others seemingly do not have as difficult a time.

If a medical disorder patient does not have a problem with the possibility of needing antidepressants as lifelong treatment and they do indeed need such a drug for emotional symptoms (and many do), they should make the decision to remain on them for as long as necessary. If at some point they want to wean off of the drug, it should be done slowly and very cautiously and never without doctor supervision.

While antidepressant medications are very helpful and necessary under the right conditions, consideration should also be given to the possibility of underlying medical causes of emotional symptoms that must also be diagnosed and treated.

When patients who are prescribed antidepressants do not adjust well to them, trials of other types of psychotropic drugs should be considered or types that are used only as-needed. Doctors can also suggest therapies or refer patients for other specific therapy treatments including Cognitive Behavioral Therapy.

Chapter 5.

More Patent Education and Doctor Communication about SSRI Antidepressants

In this chapter, I wish to express some further opinions about SSRI antidepressants in-general, that come from my years of correspondence with both doctors and patients on the subject and from several years of extensive online search on the subject.

What an amazing subject SSRI antidepressants are, with so many controversies and conflicting opinions out there about them! It is an interesting subject however and one I've searched and researched on many occasions since the year 2003. My searching was also prompted by the fact that I had five Doctors in succession try to prescribe SSRI antidepressants to me, early into my own treatment for hypothyroidism because of my experiencing some unresolved symptoms after treatment with thyroid hormone replacement therapy.

The Everything Anxiety-Coping Book!

These Doctors felt that the thyroid hormone therapy I was taking for hypothyroidism was always highly successful in all patients and that my unresolved symptoms must have been psychosomatic or simply emotionally-related ones. Once I received the correct dose of thyroid medication however, the symptoms they claimed were psychosomatic resolved significantly over time. In the mean time, I researched about SSRI antidepressant drugs because with my experience and that I was hearing from so many other fellow-patients who were continually being suggested or prescribed SSRI drugs by their Doctors, I simply had to know more about why they were being prescribed so commonly.

Let me say again, that I sincerely believe these drugs do have a purpose and that there are people who greatly benefit from them. At times they have actually prevented suicides, as some patients will attest.

On the other side of the coin however, is the fact that Doctors fall into the habit of prescribing these type drugs at every turn so-to-speak because they have been convinced of their widespread compatibility by the pharmaceutical companies who manufacture them.

Some Doctors fail to recognize the fact that there are those people the drugs might not be compatible with, who experience adverse reactions to them. Some of these type reactions have included suicidal tendencies. While this is not common, the FDA now requires mention of this possibility on the labels of these drugs. I feel with the possibility of severe side effects, patients or the parents of patients (if they are minors) that are prescribed SSRI antidepressants should be thoroughly monitored while adjusting to the drugs and sufficiently educated about them, when they are first prescribed.

I feel they should also have a hotline to their Doctors when starting these type drugs and told to report the first signs of threatening or severe side effects. Doctors should also be more willing to carefully switch patients to a different type medication if one has adverse effects, rather than telling the patient that the side effects are imagined or a sign that their emotions were on the verge of getting worse but caught just in time and that they were simply needing a dose increase of the SSRI drug.

Doctors don't always thoroughly inform patients about these possible adverse or negative possibilities because they are routinely briefed by the pharmaceutical companies who insist that the drugs can be mass-prescribed with very little chance of any adverse effects in the population of those they are administered to.

There are caring, compassionate people who work-for and head the companies who manufacture psychotropic drugs but a main driving force behind them is marketing and sales (market shares). Again, this does not take away from the fact that the drugs are greatly beneficial to many of people they are prescribed to but prescribing-abuse is also a reality with some of these types of drugs, among a small percent of doctors. There is balance needed between manufacturers and doctors because one represents marketing, while the other represents a calling to heal and preserve the lives and best health-interests of the end-recipient patients.

The reason the FDA has had to step in and require stricter measures in regard to the warnings on labels of SSRI drugs, is because severe, adverse reactions were occurring in some patients taking them and the manufacturers of the drugs did not want a great deal of press in regard to this fact.

Some even fought legally to keep from having to add warnings about adverse reactions on the prescription drug labels.

There are actually several areas of concern, including those mentioned above, in regard to SSRI antidepressants that simply require more doctor and patient education and communication. Patients in need of a trial of one of these drugs may not have the energy to read a long patient print out, that is offered with the medication so they need their doctor to brief them on all areas of concern in regard to the drugs. One example in this area is the fact that some SSRI drugs and other types of antidepressants require patients who take them to abstain from alcohol, to prevent adverse reactions but this is a warning their Doctors may fail to inform them about.

In regard to the potential for SSRI drug to lower thyroid hormones in the body, in some people who take them, I actually read about this possibility years ago, in articles published on reputable medical research websites, after I was diagnosed with thyroid disease. The fact that some of these drugs can indeed do this was included in medical research articles and not just the opinion of non-medical people. In people who take thyroid hormone replacement, this may result in a need to raise their hormone medication dose.

In people who aren't clinically hypothyroid however, taking an SSRI long term, might present the need for them to have their thyroid hormone levels tested every few months, to see if they are a patient whose levels are significantly affected by the drug. Most patient's, own bodies will adjust their thyroid hormone levels if the drug lowers them over time but this might not be true in all cases, especially in elderly patients.

Here again, is a need for Doctor and patient education about the possible reactions caused by these drugs.

If I were to sum up my opinion on the subject of prescribed psychotropic drugs, I would say that I believe many people are greatly helped by them but I also believe some people have adverse reactions to them. I believe because of this, Doctors need to brief patients better about these type facts I have addressed, rather than assuming they are safe and effective for all patients, in all cases. Certainly the only way to know if a patient will benefit who is legitimately determined to be in need of a psychotropic drug, is to place them on a trial of one. They are powerful drugs however and in my opinion, it is extremely important that doctors and patients become better educated about them and that they communicate adequately in regard to them.

Chapter 6.

Stress Management to Aid Treatments for Mind and Emotions

Stress can continually be a major problem in a person's life especially in these days of living in this crazy, hectic, fast-paced world. Stress can be brought on and aggravated by many things both major and minor including the following.

- work

- personal life problems

- financial issues

- relationships

- school

- children

- health problems

Many times stress builds from an overload of all these things combined. Some people even become stressed over the little things such as traffic, a long line at the grocery store, house chores and upcoming events or even because a waiter treated them badly at a restaurant. These are just a few examples of common stressors and there are many things that cause stress in people's lives that can accumulate and become harmful over time.

There are many stress-relievers available for practice to help us deal with the "stressors" of daily life. Yoga and meditation are very popular ways that can help us experience some relief from the stressors of a hectic life. Exercise in general is also a great way to deal with excessive stress. Having an occasional quiet time can also provide some stress reduction, by removing ourselves from everything and everyone for a few minutes each day, for some quiet, alone time. This can help us to calm-down and place us back into focus.

The Everything Anxiety-Coping Book!

Deep breathing exercises are another good way to relieve stress, by taking, slow, long, deep breaths, inflating your diaphragm (stomach), rather than your chest.

Some people suffer stress that is severe enough that they need the help of a therapist to deal with it. This can actually be a good idea if one is suffering stress severe enough that they begin to lose the ability to handle it well on their own or it is causing them emotional problems. Hobbies and leisure activities that are enjoyed can also be stress relievers. Activities involving art projects, such as painting, drawing, building things, scrapbooking, and gardening are a few simple ways to get one's mind off of all the stressors being experienced and to enjoy some leisure time.

The consequences of not mastering or at least improving the skill of stress management may include health problems, depression, and lack of sleep to name a few. Stress can contribute-to or can even be a cause of these health issues that can be potentially harmful if it is not brought under reasonable control.

The Everything Anxiety-Coping Book!

Other health problems caused-by or contributed-to by stress may also include the following.

• muscle tension

• increased heart rate

• headaches

• increased blood pressure (hypertension)

• increased risk for heart attack and stroke

• more vulnerability to colds and viruses

• increased risk for developing certain types of diseases

Stress can also take away much of the happiness in life and cause symptoms of anxiety and an increased susceptibility to depression. For these reasons it is very important to work on skills for mastering it over time (usually a lifelong pursuit and practice).

Other ways for gaining stress management would include identifying all of the things that stress you out and to begin working on improving these areas. A simple method for helping to identify stressors is to write them down in a notebook each time you find yourself getting stressed about something. This will help you to identify those stressors, so that you can begin to work on ways to better deal with and to reduce them and to possibly even eliminate them over time. Also, try working on ways to stop any negative thought patterns that contribute to stress as soon as they begin coming into your mind. Try to think positively no matter what situation may arise because it is very likely that your concerns are not as serious as you have allowed yourself to think or believe they are.

You have to develop a practice of controlling your negative responses to stressful thoughts and learn to better cope with them.

Also try to remove yourself from any situations that cause added stress for you, whether it is certain job situations or even a relationship that causes you undue stress. If you can identify anything that is negatively affecting your daily life, it is important to remove yourself from those things if at all possible, since they will only serve to make life more difficult and complicated than it should reasonably have to be.

Most people can benefit in many ways from mastering these skills for reducing stress which can lend toward a much happier and healthier life. The benefits of better health that can result are not only physical but also mental and emotional. Mastering these skills can also help you to benefit more from life itself and help you to experience more enjoyment as well.

Hopefully more people will begin to realize that chronic stress is a continually growing problem in our society and may actually cause negative and violent behaviors in some people.

The Everything Anxiety-Coping Book!

We all must begin working on skills and methods for coping because stress can easily spiral out of control if we do not do everything we can to control it instead of allowing it to control us.

People experiencing the emotional or mental disorders discussed within the preceding chapters and their family, friends and associates, should become aware of how commonly these disorders can co-exist (stress, anxiety and depression). They should also learn about the major features that help to distinguish between them and about the available treatments that can restore an improved quality of life to the sufferers of them.

(END)

www.ingramcontent.com/pod-product-compliance
Lightning Source LLC
Chambersburg PA
CBHW030302290526
45785CB00001B/178